THE CONTAINER GARDENER

THE CONTAINER GARDENER

RUPERT GOLBY

Photographs by Andrew Lawson and Jerry Harpur

Stemmer House

PUBLISHERS, INC.

Owings Mills, Maryland

Special material for US edition © 1995 by Stemmer House Publishers, Inc.
First published in the United States in 1995 by Stemmer House Publishers, Inc.

Inquiries are to be directed to Stemmer House Publishers, Inc.
2627 Caves Road
Owings Mills, Maryland 21117
A Barbara Holdridge book

Library of Congress Cataloging-in-Publication Data

Golby, Rupert.
    The container gardener / Rupert Golby : photographs by Andrew
Lawson and Jerry Harpur.
        p.   cm.
    Originally published: London : Headline Book Pub., 1993.
    Includes bibliographical references (p.   ) and index.
    ISBN 0-88045-129-7 : $ 35.00
    1. Container gardening.   2. Container gardening — Great Britain.
3. Plant containers.   I. Title.
SB418.G65   1995
717 — dc20   94-24264
                                                                      CIP

AN EDDISON·SADD EDITION
Edited, designed and produced by
Eddison Sadd Editions Limited
St Chad's Court
146B King's Cross Road
London WC1X 9DH

Phototypeset in Caslon Old Face by
Servis Filmsetting Limited, Manchester, England
Origination by Scantrans, Singapore
Printing and binding by
Artes Graficas Toledo, SA in Spain
DLTO: 1440–1994

Illustration on page 1. *Spring at the Old Rectory is marked by bulbs –
tulips in particular – bursting into flower. Here they surround a dome of
clipped box in a wooden tub, artfully festooned with swags of ivy. (p.139)*

Illustration on page 2. Convolvulus elegantissimus *enlivens the muted leaf
colours of purple sage and hebe which reflects the patina of age formed
on the lead container. (p.156)*

CONTENTS

THE MAKING OF A CLASSIC POT

The Container Gardener *grew out of* The Terracotta Gardener *and, like all good garden projects, while growing it has been much pruned, grafted and even hybridized.*

It was decided early on that this second volume should widen the choice of containers to include stone, metal and wood, as well as terracotta, and that more use should be made of the seasons to encourage unusual plantings. As I felt ill-equipped to write this more plant-orientated book, my friend and personal plant advisor Rupert Golby agreed to take on the task. Rupert had helped me with The Terracotta Gardener *as well as agreeing to be one of its contributors. As a professional horticulturist and garden designer he knows more about plants and container growing, in particular, than I do. But it is my pleasure to introduce this new book.*

JIM KEELING

Opposite. *The classic pot, richly decorated with cornucopia and acanthus leaves, is raised above mere flowerpots in the selling yard of Whichford Pottery. It is planted permanently with a standard variegated holly.*

A New Beginning

Originally, I thought I would run swiftly through garden history, pointing out what containers were used and when, and what plants were put in them, something like: Egyptian and Roman – ivy and myrtle; medieval – herbs and topiary; Renaissance onwards – citrus fruit; seventeenth century – 'exotic greens'; nineteenth century – use of half-hardy bedding. I tried, but the Muses would not inspire me. Instead I switched back to the containers themselves, and began re-tracing the old forms. That set me thinking. How extraordinary that the most popular urns sold by modern garden centres still bear the same motifs used by the Romans two-thousand years ago.

So I decided to write my introduction not so much on *what* the old forms and plants were, but *why* they were used, to point out the forgotten iconography of what today we take for granted. To do this, I shall tell the story of one particular pot, the one shown on page 6. It is a really big flowerpot, several feet across and full of the old motifs – the sort of thing we associate with the Villa d'Este and the Boboli gardens in Italy, or Blenheim Palace, England. This is the story of how I came to make this pot.

I had already been a potter for a dozen years before I felt confident enough to try this pot. These large pots are difficult technically, and they test your sense of proportion and composition rather more noticeably than smaller ones.

I was by then a good 'thrower', able to construct big pots from several sections on the potter's wheel, so this project marked a new beginning. I was fresh back from studying in Italy and my mind was full, not of the plain-banded orange pots (of which I already made a simple version on the wheel), but of those magnificent Italian urns festooned with fruit and guarded by strange heads. I could not possibly throw such a complex pot on the wheel. I would have to make it by beating clay into a mould, and to get the mould I must first make up an original to cast. So, armed with a few photographs of old Italian examples, I began.

But where to begin? I scanned my sketchbook, peered at the amateur photographs. Then I returned to the pottery with a lump of clay and some modelling tools, a board to rest on. Uneasily I looked again at the illustrations. From of all the pots I liked the most, there leered the same face. I knew enough about Greek and Roman mythology to recognize a satyr, and I felt distinctly uncomfortable in his presence. Satyrs represent untamed nature, and hence licence and lust. They are anciently related to Pan, having human heads and torsos, with the horns, beard and legs of a goat.

I worked long and hard on that head, and I like it now as well as anything I have ever made. My satyr is wrinkled, old as Pan himself, and his eyes twinkle wickedly beneath his curling horns.

The following day I began on two other horns – the two cornucopia, or horns of plenty, either

A festive satyr decorates an eighteenth-century lead urn, after the designs in James Gibbs' Book of Architecture, *first published 1728.*

In the early morning light, Jim Keeling's wrinkled old satyr leers at passers-by. From the sides of his beard sprout cornucopia.

side of the satyr. The same horns? At the time I was swept along, modelling whatever caught my eye in old pots, and only recently have I begun looking into what these designs actually stand for. There is much more to them than I had supposed.

Cornucopia were always associated with satyrs and the rites of Dionysus, but they were originally a gift to Amaltheia. She was a goat-nymph who lived in Crete on Mount Dicte, and had the honour of suckling the infant Zeus. Some say that it was her skin which became the *aegis* that protected Zeus and Athene, and was later borrowed by Achilles. Her horns were blessed with endless abundance, becoming the cornucopia. They were adopted, in their hollow, receptive female form, by all the deities of vegetation and fate, and mother goddesses such as Demeter and Fortuna. Not to be outdone, Priapus also claimed

them as his. Turning them over he made versions of his usual crude phallus, promising the male version of endless fecundity.

A Forgotten Symbolism

I began my Italian urns quite unaware that each element can tell us so much of the deities who protected and fertilized the gardens of the Ancients. Since the Renaissance, our culture has become increasingly one-dimensional in how it views the world. This is in sharp contrast with earlier times, when people would expect to 'read' any manufactured object almost as we now read a well-argued book; each detail pointing symbolically to a second, unseen world.

Thus in medieval Christian art and architecture, representations of nature were codified and given a second, symbolic meaning. In the Islamic world, where the representation of living forms was forbidden by the teachings of the Koran, this same movement to direct the observer to an unseen reality through the use of ordinary objects was reflected in the ever-more ingenious use of lettering. Quotations from the scriptures were used by calligraphers, architects, and even potters as decoration, the interwoven scripts becoming so complex that the unravelling of their meaning was in itself a difficult meditation.

My satyr now lay grinning up at me on the modelling board, a cornucopia sprouting from each side of his beard. Next, I composed a medley of fruit to spill from their gaping mouths. I should really have been more careful, for the shape of each fruit carries its own message. I chose apples, quinces, oranges, pears and grapes. I made up the swag from sections of real fruit with clay squeezed into the gaps. My apple trees were raided for small, well-formed fruit. The quinces were Japanese, and the oranges came from the local shop. The whole construction was daubed with plaster to make a cast. Then, when the plaster was dry, a mess of squashed fruit was gouged from its casing.

If I had looked more closely at antique swags, I should have included a pomegranate. These strange fruits sprang from the blood of Dionysus and, with their myriad seeds, they offer a counterpoint to the serene unity of Aphrodite's apple. Both fruits have their dark associations: it was an apple, the Apple of Discord, which Paris gave to Aphrodite rather than to Hera or Athene, thus causing the Trojan war; and the seeds of a pomegranate were used by Pluto to trick Persephone, binding her to Hades for a third of the year, and so bringing Winter. In general, however, all fruit stands for fertility and abundance.

After the fruit came leaves. On the rim of the pot I chose to put oak leaves, which, given the difficulty of finishing these vast pots without their falling apart or blowing up in the early stages of firing, was suitably hopeful. Zeus claims the oak for it is strong and durable; and so crowns of oak leaves have always stood for courage in adversity and victory. Round the base of the pot were to grow acanthus leaves, more like the stylized versions on Corinthian columns than those in my garden. Like grapes, which give the 'wine of life', acanthus in Mediterranean countries has always stood for immortality, and was often planted on graves. Perhaps it is because its leaves outline the horns of the reborn crescent moon. Finally I modelled some rope above and below the acanthus leaves, to tie all these pieces together.

If I was remodelling my urn now, I might change two things. There is a half-roundel of a flower that I have not mentioned which could stand for Flora, who gave birth to the flowers of spring after cavorting with Zephrus, the West Wind, but I feel that no garden Pantheon is complete without full tribute to Demeter. Her corn and barley are some of the oldest of all symbols, signifying renewal of life, resurrection and fertility. Made into bread, they stand, with wine, for the balanced product of human labour on earth. Grain even became, in the Eleusinian Mysteries, an object of deep mystical contemplation: 'the ear of corn that had been reaped in silence'. So next time I shall replace the binding ropes with plaits of corn and barley. From the tip of the satyr's beard sprouts one last diminutive cornucopia with only three fruits. It neatly fills a gap, but somehow adds nothing. In future I shall

A lidded vase by Jane Hogben, decorated with cherubs playing among trailing vines, stands in Helen Preston's garden. (p.33)

change it to a satyr's magic staff, entwined with ivy and a knot of ribbons, and surmounted by a pine cone, which he could use on his wild rampages around my customers' gardens.

If I were not so keen on remembering the old deities, I could replace, as the Italians often do, my satyr with a lion. We still seem to choose the old protectors for our gardens, and lions are obvious candidates for their fiery strength. They were also believed to sleep with their eyes open. If, on a pot, the lion holds a ring in its jaws (replacing the satyr's cornucopia as a start for swags of fruit) it is in its role as Guardian of the Way: its mouth gaping like the gates of the underworld, the ring as the Door of Deliverance for the soul. This motif often appears on the side of stone urns with drapes of funeral winding sheet between; slightly morbid unless the top of the lid is decorated with the flames of resurrection.

I have also seen the four satyrs replaced by the winged heads of cherubs. After the many-eyed Seraphim, Cherubim rank second in the nine orders of angels, and as a foursome they would represent the four elemental powers guarding the Garden of Paradise, of which more later.

MAKING THE POT

Having cast a mould from each detail of the decoration, I next set about making the body of the pot itself. In the centre of my workshop I fixed an old scaffold pole, a kind of *axis mundi*, joining the sky and earth, round which my old gods could circle. About this I heaped bricks to make a central core and covered them with a great pile of clay to make my mould. Then I joined a template, the outline of the pot-to-be, to my pole and pushed it around, forcing the mound of clay to take on the shape of the pot I desired. Onto this solid core I fixed my decoration, piece by piece. By the time every detail was in place to my satisfaction, a week had passed. This left the daunting task of committing the finished mould to plaster; and from the mould gained I would finally make the first pot.

A mould of this size – over three foot high and four foot across, weighing several hundredweight – needs to be made in sections. I chose to have eight sections covering the sides of the pot, with a giant ring locking the top together and covering the rim.

When the day came to take the finished mould apart, my helpers and I laid the pieces in order outside, where they steamed in the sun. Each one needed fettling, the rough edges and undercuts carving away. It took a week to dry the mould. Then we assembled it to make the first pot, binding the pieces together with rope. First the decorations were filled with clay, then coils of clay were beaten round and up the sides and smoothed to an even thickness.

The first two attempts collapsed as we removed the mould. So we left the third in the mould until the following day, to allow the dry plaster to suck moisture from the wet clay. But clay shrinks as it dries, and by morning huge cracks appeared in the pot, before it had even been uncovered. Our fourth effort was, at last, successful. We removed only the upper parts of the mould, and propped the damp rim as we went. The following day the last parts of the mould were removed, and I had my first sight of a finished pot – finished, that is, apart from the filling of blemishes, touching up of the moustaches, putting on of extra leaves, cutting out under horns and so on; the small details that bring a press-moulded pot to life.

There followed six weeks of nursing. Any draught or excess of heat, and a crack would appear. So it was, in fact, many pots before a perfect version presented itself before the kiln.

As for the kiln, to be frost-proof the pots must be heated until they become the colour of glowing wheatstraw, 1000°C (1832°F). I had to make a special kiln for my big pots, firing them over five slow days.

I still get a thrill of pleasure each time I see one of these huge pots come out of the kiln, and the first one that ever emerged, battered and cracked though it was, filled me with delight. For some time it sat impressively outside the pottery. Spring came, and it began to look reproachfully empty. Sooner or later I would have to plant it up. Over the years I have tried many different things. Now I feel that having made a pot so full of classical allusions I should try to fill it with flowers which tell the same sorts of stories.

THE PLANTS OF LIFE AND DEATH

Through the eyes of the Ancients, plants led to the world of the gods. They grew, surely, by some mystical power, and in their cycle of birth, growth, death and rebirth they mirrored the immortality of the human soul. For this reason, flower gardens have always been associated with Paradise or the Elysian Fields. The exact attribution of a plant to a deity or mood can happen for a number of reasons. The shape of the leaf or flower, the number of petals or the form of the plant may be suggestive. Different colours mean many different things, and heavy scent will permeate even to the underworld, which is probably why we still send flowers to a funeral.

Which puts me in mind to start with plants of sombre meaning. In ancient Greece, the dead were often buried in sacred groves, and cypress trees with their haunting smell, loved by Hades, still grow in cemeteries. Although poppies are symbols of fecundity, and as such are woven into the hair of all great mother deities, they also represent sleep and oblivion, and so are the emblem of these gods, Hypnos and Morpheus. The bitterness of death could be represented by wormwood, held by warlike Ares. Add colour from the spilt blood of gods and heroes: red anemones from the gored Adonis; purple violets from Attis; and blue hyacinths from Hyacinthus, a beautiful youth loved by both Apollo and Zephrus. One day he was playing quoits with Apollo. Zephrus was madly jealous and, when it was Apollo's turn to throw, blew so strongly that the god's quoit turned in the air and struck young Hyacinthus a deadly blow to the head. If you look at the leaf of a hyacinth, you can still see written there the exclamation of woe 'ai, ai!' or the letter upsilon, the initial of his name. For some extra colour, iris could raise her upright leaves and bright flowers. She was a messenger of the gods and would lead souls from this world to the next.

Such plants need balance from others of a more optimistic nature. A Dionysiac revel could include a gnarled pine twined with ivy and twisting vines, or Pan's alder (perhaps one with a variegated foliage) which always went with spring revels and fire festivals.

For love, I would plant a walnut tree if it were not so large. Its nuts were always served at Roman weddings, a fine example of the wry humour often present in symbols – it spoke of fertility and longevity, but also of hidden wisdom and strength in adversity (the caryatids were nut nymphs). Better perhaps to choose an old-fashioned rose growing from a carpet of single asters, both would represent Aphrodite, and a few narcissi in spring would warn of the dangers of self-love. I would try also to include some sunflowers in memory of Clytie, who turned into a sunflower when spurned by Apollo, and still slavishly follows his every move across the sky.

For my final group I leave the Ancient World. I have mentioned Greek and Roman interpretations of nature, but they were using still older myths from Egypt, Sumeria, Chaldea and elsewhere. In the same way, Christian culture has adopted and refashioned the old Classical ideas. Many of the choicest plants have ended up as symbols for the Virgin Mary, as any medieval painting will show. So I will choose from a standard apple tree, a rose or jasmine, beneath which grow a bed of white violets for the early spring, then lily-of-the-valley, and purple cyclamen for the autumn. All Aphrodite's flowers now belong to Our Lady: the iris, and, best of all, the white lily of Hera. Dante called this flower 'the Lily of Faith'. In medieval iconography, all its parts had their meaning: the straight stalk, Our Lady's godly mind; its hanging leaves, her humility; its fragrance, her sweet motherhood; its whiteness, her purity.

IN A PARADISE GARDEN

With my pot made, fired and planted, I should place it where it really belongs – in a paradise garden. Four years ago, I built a small walled secret garden between my house and the pottery. With Rupert Golby's help, it has turned into a place which everyone loves. I believe that its appeal, like that of the old motifs and flowers, lies in the use made of traditional forms that in their symbolism satisfy something deep inside us.

The original *Pairidaeza* parks were created in Persia in the centuries before Christ. They embodied the Zoroastrian ideal of a balanced communion between the four sacred elements of earth, air (scent), water and fire. The Greek word *paradisos* describes a state of blessedness, like these ideal gardens. In the first Paradise, there were two trees: one the Tree of Knowledge, the other the Tree of Life. Unfortunately, Eve took only the Apple of Knowledge. God banished Adam and Eve from the Garden of Eden not least to prevent them from eating of the Tree of Immortality, and the quest for this fruit continues to fire us all.

At the centre of a paradise garden is a fountain which represents this Tree of Life. Indeed medieval paintings often portray the fountain with a tall stem, like the trunk of a tree, with gushing rivulets springing from it like branches. The

Tree of Life stands at the cosmic centre, and from it flow the living waters of immortality, down the four paths of the garden to the four corners of the world; in the Persian originals there were actual canals down the middle of the paths.

My garden is modest in size, enclosed by high mud walls topped with old tiles. As in a medieval castle garden, coming inside this wall promises peace. It offers a protection from the 'forest' of everyday life, and the garden encourages quiet contemplation.

I find it heartening that so many people today choose to spend their time gardening. It puts back a little sanity into the world, and keeps us in touch with the earth and the annual cycle of the seasons. When we put plants in a flowerpot it is a ritual full of hope, and the promise of love, too, and care if the plants are to survive. That is how the Ancients would have perceived it, and that is why they decorated their urns with the attributes of the deities who symbolized those sides of life.

So if you happen to see a satyr scowling at you from the side of an urn, beside a fountain, or from over a mossy doorway, consider this: once, like the god Pan, his horns were plentiful and his colours of green and red were those of life itself. Somehow, by some misunderstanding, our society alienated Pan, and thrust his horns onto the head of the devil, using his colours for distrust, envy and hell. Nature became something to tame and exploit, with the dire environmental consequences which we now face. So whenever I tend my garden, and in particular plant up a flower pot and care for it from year to year, I hope that in a small way I begin to redress that imbalance.

The intimate confines of the secret garden at Whichford create an ambience full of scents and fine details, not found in larger gardens.

Part One

THE PLANTING DISPLAYS

I visit many gardens during the course of my work and I see numerous fine containers. Large horse-troughs, precisely placed in driveways, and pairs of boxes, emphasizing doorways, come to mind. Occasionally, though, elegant urns can be seen in reduced circumstances; languishing on the ground when they should be raised on piers, pedestals or wall-tops, or a myriad of small pots cluttering a terrace where one large pot would be preferable. With the help of fifteen inspired gardeners, I have tried to show containers in appropriate and important sites.

I met and talked with each of the contributors in turn. More often than not I walked with them through their gardens, discussing gardening in general as well as their ideas for the future, so when I came to write, each section would reflect a different personality.

I hope, as you look through these pages you will be tempted to recreate some of the plantings. They have been chosen to inspire and infuse new ideas, so any one pot may be adapted and experimented with in different contexts – you will find all the details you need in Part Two. I also believe, that like me, you will appreciate the forethought, skill and ingenuity employed by each of the gardeners concerned.

Opposite. *A rich tapestry of diverse plants and colours interwoven with the silvery threads of* Helichrysum petiolare *combine together to form a potted 'border', staged like a sweet shop window, in Beth Chatto's garden. (pp. 101 and 150)*

THE OLD RECTORY
Drawing-room bananas

ANNIE HUNTINGTON

The county of Northamptonshire in the heart of England is not well known for its mild gardening climate, but there lives here, near Kettering, a wonderful gardener whose enthusiasm it takes more than cold rain to dampen. For this is Annie Huntington, a lady not of these shores. Mrs Huntington was raised in Buffalo, New York State. Later she moved to New York and then to the West Indies, before coming to England and finally settling in Northamptonshire.

It was in 1984 that Mr and Mrs Huntington bought The Old Rectory, 'We started work on the gardens straight away – that's why we don't have any drawing-room curtains! Instead we have overwintering oleanders on the drawing-room window sills. When we have banana plants', Mrs Huntington's latest idea, 'perhaps we won't need curtains at all!'

It would be fair to say that the majority of container gardeners put their pots away for winter or simply leave them empty. Not Mrs Huntington. She plants for winter, but the main impact comes in early spring. What would otherwise become a bare terrace after the summer excesses of bedding have gone, is refurnished for autumn with pots of evergreen shrubs and herba-

ceous plants. In spring tulips, dwarf daffodils and iris burst into flower, paying back with interest the time spent carefully planting them on a chilly October day. 'I love tulips massed in pots, particularly the interesting colours of the viridifloras and the elegant shapes of the lily-flowered forms. To me they're as beautiful as lilies.'

In summer, the garden at The Old Rectory has subtle hints of Mrs Huntington's past. She grows *Nerium oleander*, *Bougainvillea* and *Feijoa* in large containers on the terrace to remind her of the West Indies. In the potager, designed five years ago by Rosemary Verey, traditional vegetables rub shoulders with foreign friends. Oranges and lemons fruiting in pots and, to give them their essential acid soil, blueberries (for pies) are grown in containers and watered only with rain water to avoid lime-contaminated tap water. The pots are almost encircled by the trailing growths of pumpkins (also for pies!). After a recent Mediterranean trip an olive tree can be found, enjoying the summer sun in the potager. 'In Cyprus they told me, if you dry olive branches and hang them up in the house you have no end of good luck.'

Mrs Huntington enjoys finding the rare and unusual to fill her pots, and her filing cabinet of specialist nursery catalogues is an impressive sight. Beautiful specimens of *Rhodochiton atrosanguineus* have been the centre of attention this summer, due mainly to her good idea of training their long self-clinging growths over iron globes of open hoop-like construction to allow the purple bell flowers to swing inside.

TORCH-LIKE TULIPS

Opposite. *After the familiar bursts of yellow daffodils, large-flowered tulips offer the first real chance to influence the colour schemes of spring.* (p.139)

The main area for displaying pots is a small west-facing courtyard by the kitchen door where stone cobbles make an excellent surface for showing off plants and containers alike. This summer Mrs Huntington's terracotta pots froth with pelargoniums. I comment on her use of terracotta. 'Well there's no alternative really. In an ideal world I would always buy old stone and lead urns but we cannot afford to do that, particularly as I like a lot of containers around the garden. I also feel this is a good house but not a grand house, and so containers shouldn't be over elaborate. The containers you buy have to be put in perspective with the house, even though you may love sweeping swan or fallen angel decoration.' She feels it is important to have a degree of uniformity in the containers, rather than be tempted to buy as many styles and materials as possible.

'We brought no end of those pretty, brightly glazed Spanish pots back from Seville – you never saw anything like the car or the aeroplane on our way back! However they were not in the least frost hardy and so when they got caught by the first frost, that was the end of them. The main objection to them, though, was the fact that they didn't look right in England. They were totally out of keeping with this house.'

Other codes of practice followed at the Old Rectory include using plain pots full of lilies or verbenas dropped into 'black holes' which appear in the borders, where oriental poppies or dicentras have disappeared earlier in the season. And Mrs Huntington insists that 'You've got to rotate them,' by turning the container on the spot from time to time, to give the back of a pot a turn at the front, and so keep a more even distribution of growth and flowers. Pots are also swapped around, giving each pot a period of sun, semi-shade, then sun again.

Although the potager contains many herbs, Mrs Huntington is never without a large pot of herbs by the back door. 'A mixture of herbs can look terribly pretty, and by the back door they provide instant access for the cook . . . me in other words!'

EASTER-DAY WELCOME

Opposite. *These pots are so full they could rival many a summer display, and it is hard to believe they have stood the vagaries of a Northamptonshire winter. The marbled leaves of* Silybum marianum *look good enough to eat!* (p.139)

ORANGE POTS AND LEMONS

Above. *One of several citrus trees in the potager, this small but well-shaped young lemon tree,* Citrus limon, *bears fruit surprisingly early in its life. It stands at the end of box-edged brick and concrete paths.*

ARISTOCRATIC LILIES

Above. *A collection of pots outside the back door is dominated by the unashamedly showy* Lilium *'Capitol'. Lilies need a deep container to give them stability and accommodate the stem roots, which grow six inches above the bulb.* (p.139)

BELLE GLOBES

Opposite. *A painted iron-work globe fitted over a large half-pot makes the ideal climbing frame for twining* Rhodochiton atrosanguineus *to display its intriguing bell-like flowers, so often hidden when grown upright.* (p.139)

SOUVENIR FROM SEVILLE

Above. *This stone step has a surprise in its corner — a brightly coloured, highly glazed pot from Spain. Perhaps more at home indoors than on a country-house terrace, it has been planted with* Scaevola aemula *'Blue Fan', brilliant in flower.*

FLOWERY FILLER

Opposite. *Herbaceous plants such as Oriental poppies or, in this case,* Fritillaria persica *'Adiyaman' tend to die away after flowering early in summer. To fill unsightly gaps, Annie Huntingdon plants extra pots of tender perennials which can be relied upon for plenty of flowers and colour from late May onwards. When the fritillary stems have withered, they are cleared away and a large flowerpot full of pelargoniums and argyranthemums fills the space. (p.140)*

A HAPPY CHANCE

Above. *Tulips, narcissus and dicentra give a pleasing display of delicate colours and flower shapes. Some people may say a single mass of one cultivar of tulip or daffodil would be more dramatic than a mixture of plants. When three different plants with short flowering periods are brought together the chance of their peaking as one is unpredictable; but when they do the effect is memorable. The large unclipped bush of variegated box stands alone in winter. Periwinkle was to have trailed over the edge of the pot, but winter weather proved too hard and it did not survive. (p.140)*

BARNSLEY HOUSE

Don't be dull . . . try everything in pots

ROSEMARY VEREY

Rosemary Verey uses many containers in her beautiful Gloucestershire garden to furnish terrace and temple, veranda and vegetable garden, conservatory and any empty corners. Rosemary's diversity of plantings and planters are worth close examination whether you visit her garden in January or July. There is always something of interest to note down in your pocket note book, a must for visiting this garden if only to remember the concoctions of herbaceous and bedding plants. (Rosemary has been known to offer pencil and paper to those who ask questions and only make mental notes.)

Where large containers are needed Rosemary tends to resort to wooden half-barrels or, occasionally, the elegant wooden Versailles boxes designed by her son Charles. I ask her about the row of four wooden barrels prominently placed on the main terrace in front of the house and dare to suggest that they may not be good enough for such a position. Instantly Rosemary challenges me to find a departing visitor who can recall the type of container used on her terrace: 'It's the plants they will have noticed, not the container they are in. We always plant just one pelargo-nium in the centre of each tub. They must be one-year-old plants grown on from cuttings taken the previous year, then they grow really well the following year. This is the pelargonium we call 'Best Mauve'; it's so good, don't you think?' These trailing, ivy-leaved pelargoniums are tied up onto tripods of bamboo canes which enable them to attain a height of three-and-a-half foot, and they display a mass of blooms continuously from May to October.

It is true, the tubs themselves are hardly noticeable as, with age, they have become silvery grey and merge with the paving. What one does notice, however, is that the size and scale of the tubs is proportionally correctly with the terrace. For winter these tubs are planted with variegated hollies grown as standard specimens, hebes, vinca, primulas and forget-me-nots, under-planted with spring flowering bulbs of tulips, narcissus, iris and crocus, planted in layers. The tubs contribute greatly to the appearance of the terrace during these bleak months when the winter-sweet, *Chimonanthus praecox*, is the only shrub there plucky enough to join in with a winter display of its own, its candle-wax col-oured, starry flowers powerfully scenting the entire area.

Many containers are gathered together in the shelter of the classic eighteenth-century temple, rescued from neglect and vandalism in the grounds of Fairford Park and re-erected as a summer house by Rosemary and her late husband David at Barnsley. The back wall is cleanly white-washed creating a plain back-drop for the

A WELL-FURNISHED TERRACE

Opposite. *One of four oak half-barrels placed on the main terrace, it overflows with tender plants, and a central wig-wam support is smothered with the pelargonium 'Best Mauve'. Behind, attractively planted pots crowd the door steps.* (p.140)

colourful mixture of plants. We stood back, taking in the powerful colours. 'We don't normally allow strong reds into the garden, and certainly not with the really strong pink of *Maurandya erubescens* and blues and blue-reds of other flowers. In theory they should clash violently. Against the stark white background they manage to mellow together.'

We make our way back across the garden. It is late summer and a perennial sweet pea, rich pink in colour twines its way through a dark purple-leaved berberis giving beautiful tonal contrast. In front cosmos and cleomes mingle with one another; their colours remind me of a plate of iced cakes. Rosemary has an impressively wide knowledge of plants, but her understanding of how best to use them is, I think, her greatest strength. In many cases plants one would not normally associate with one another are here grown together to produce dramatic, stunning or sometimes amusing effects. Whatever reaction they provoke, they stimulate interest and draw comment from the most reluctant of gardeners.

We reach the herb knot, a geometric pattern of dwarf box hedges with diamond-shaped and triangular compartments each filled with herbs. This feature epitomizes the style of gardening adopted by Rosemary. She loves the shapes created by the formal features she first discovered in her collection of period gardening books. Her garden is littered with clipped box balls and fancifully fashioned hedges, and it is difficult to believe that this has all been created in just thirty years. She and her husband created the individual areas, dividing them with borders of mixed shrubs and perennials, in such a way that the house and garden are well balanced and in harmony with one another.

Our walk continues on to the pillared conservatory, across a small stone terrace where massed ranks of containers seem ready to defend the glass palace to the end. Sitting beneath long festoons of the cup-and-saucer flower, *Cobaea scandens*, we talk of plants and containers. 'One plant that has been a huge success with me is this wonderful *Pelargonium* 'Lady Plymouth'. She's been looking

absolutely tremendous for nearly three years now. I love her dearly.' Growing beside her, trailing from a stone trough on the back wall of the conservatory, are two tender salvias, *S. involucrata* 'Bethellii' and *S. grahamii*.

My eye wanders to a plastic pot nearby with good foliage tumbling over its sides. Rosemary catches my sideways glance proclaiming, 'Look at that, there couldn't be anything more satisfactory than that ladder fern with its dark green leaves and the very pale lime green, chartreuse green almost, of *Pelargonium* 'Golden Crest'. I hate the plastic pot, though; its like wearing something that came from the penny stores rather than the couturier. A container made from a natural material becomes more beautiful with age; it grows in charm – plastic becomes scruffy.'

Other plants grown in containers and much admired by Rosemary are the lemon verbenas, *Aloysia triphylla*, trained as standard plants and clipped back hard each April before new growth commences. These are grown in half-barrels, surrounded at their feet by diascias for the summer. Shallow terracotta seed pans are made into gardens in miniature by placing a tiny standard box ball centrally and edged with a symmetrical pattern of thyme in its green, gold and variegated forms.

In August and September, the bridal wreath, *Francoa sonchifolia*, puts on a show. Beloved by Gertrude Jekyll for its usefulness, this plant is also a favourite of Rosemary's. Placed in containers either side of steps and along balustrading, its long wand-like flowers of pale pink gently lean out towards the sun.

As I left Rosemary she gave the subject a final broadside shot: 'Don't be dull, try anything and everything in pots!'

PANS OF THYME

Opposite. *Herbs, including thyme, chives and germander, can be grown in shallow pans such as salting troughs and low pans. Here thyme in different variegations is used to make patterns around a central tiny standard box ball. (p.141)*

FOLIAGE FORMS

Opposite. *The different colours and forms of foliage alone create delightful contrasts. Dark plumes of bronze fennel stand against Mr Bowles' golden grass only to be reflected back in the purple tints of* Viola labradorica. *(p.141)*

SPRING ARRIVES

Above. *An open expanse of winter rain-washed terrace is enlivened by the first signs of spring. The standard holly, still young, is old enough to give winter interest. (p.141)*

A FLOURISH OF TRUMPETS

Left. *A welcoming fanfare of angel's trumpets, or daturas, greet visitors to Rosemary's front door. The large, pure white, pendulous flowers resemble artificial decorations hung up just for the day.* (p.141)

MULTI-STOREY BULBS

Above. *In spring the Barnsley House barrels are bursting with a succession of flowering bulbs. They are planted in autumn in layers. At the lowest level go the large bulbs of tulips and narcissus; above these, just three inches beneath the compost surface, are* Iris reticulata *and early crocus.* (p.142)

A FULHAM TOWN HOUSE

An oasis of vegetation

HELEN PRESTON

small garden in a town or city is an important ingredient in this book of otherwise rather grand, large country-house gardens. A garden in London would fit the bill, I thought. So it was that one very warm July morning, I found myself sitting in a garden just off the King's Road surrounded by a profusion of plants, a perfect oasis of vegetation in an otherwise hostile environment. I had come to meet Helen Preston, a busy executive, who for the past three years has run 'Thomas Goode', the china and glass store in South Audley Street. Her tiny garden gives her immeasurable pleasure and a wonderful escape from the many daily decisions she has to make.

Helen and her husband have lived here for fifteen years. They finally decided the garden was too small for a lawn, having tried in one area but the heavy shade cast by a large sycamore growing in a neighbouring garden made it impossible. So the whole garden was paved and divided into two equal parts, the far end raised by two steps to give a little more interest. Narrow borders were left around the sides and five-foot high walls were erected to replace post and wire fences. A border

SUMMER FIREWORKS

Opposite. *Rich coloured plants reflect the washed tones and luscious grapes which decorate this pot. The multi-coloured foliage of* Berberis thunbergii *'Harlequin' is dominant and the fading heads of* Allium christophii *burst above, like fireworks.* (p.142)

was also left along the top of the level change to divide the garden visually. With the paved surface areas and the dominating house and garden walls, the borders were to be important in creating a softening lush greenery.

Helen has always enjoyed gardens, even in childhood. And she says of her parent's garden of traditional vegetables and fruit with herbaceous borders of delphiniums, lupins and peonies: 'As a small child I loved picking the flowers and arranging them in big vases.' Other influences come from friends who are keen gardeners and from newspaper and magazine articles which she devours hungrily. 'I always think one of the great things in life is knowing what to copy. My sort of gardening is very much trial and error, I always overplant because I can never believe anything is ever going to grow. Consequently I spend a lot of time replanting or pruning and removing to keep some sort of order!'

Helen's container gardening was originally forced on her out of necessity as a previous house had no garden, just a balcony-come-rooftop. 'So it was containers or nothing. I planted them with pelargoniums, lobelia and alyssum. When I moved here I realized how crashingly boring this was, so I decided on clashing mixtures of pink, lilac and orange. That was fun for a while, but it all got a bit much so I went to the other extreme and planted only white flowers. Then I bought the book *The Terracotta Gardener* which has totally revolutionized my pot-planting life. It was so marvellous seeing the extraordinary plantings and all those funny things growing together. I actually made up some of the plantings using the plans at the back of the book.

'We now rent a cottage down in Gloucestershire where I have what passes as a terrace, made of sloping concrete, running along the south side of the house. It is quite ugly but, as we don't own the cottage, I was not about to start digging it up. The only thing to do was to cover much of the concrete with pots. This we have done and to huge aesthetic benefit to the house.'

Helen finds her friend Kenneth Turner's shop a great source of inspiration, originality and humour. 'He gives you a jolt, by using many refreshingly different things together. Earlier this year he grew five huge white *Amaryllis* in square glass containers filled with beautifully rounded pebbles; it looked stunning. He has also made a pair of flower-pot men which stand either side of the shop entrance. One has nasturtiums planted in his hat, the other with an armful of nasturtiums which cascade down to the ground.

'Another source of inspiration to me is a wonderfully creative close friend and colleague, Tom Ellery. He has a flat and garden in Little Venice, which is bounded by high brick walls completely clothed by sheets of ivy and cascading roses and clematis. Among all this growth you catch sight of thrusts of colour here and there and realize these are bedding plants grown in pots, either suspended from high on the wall or perched on ledges. Mostly masses of pink or white, they merge with the background climbing plants, and give detail to the great arching sprays of the climbers, which is very effective. It's wonderful having people around you who keep giving you fresh ideas and a different way of looking at things.'

Helen uses many pots made by ceramic sculptor Jane Hogben. Her pots are hand-built using coiling techniques with press-moulded cherubs and vines applied to give elaborate high-relief decoration. Before firing the pots, Jane applies diluted slips to give a pale wash of different tones to mimic the subtle weathering of old terracotta which gives the pots an air of antiquity when still relatively new.

A narrow alley runs along the side of the garden room to a French window into the sitting-room. 'I thought simple metal arches spanning the alley and covered with a profusion of clematis and roses would contrast well with lines of topiary-filled pots. The idea of topiary in this position came from Kenneth Turner's garden where he has a similar alley. I thought the box shapes looked absolutely stunning. In my garden they make the alley look wider than it is and not like a pokey little side passage.'

From her table and chairs on the lower level of paving we move into the garden dining-room, almost bare of pots and plants. Helen likes it this way so as not to distract from the garden beyond. 'If I did have some planting in here it would be something very simple which did not compete with the garden.' The large windows give a pleasing outlook. Roses clamber up walls, trellis and arbour. One ambitious 'Mermaid' rose has triumphed in reaching the top windows of the house; only to be scrambled over by a presumptuous *Solanum jasminoides* 'Album' which showers clusters of starry, pure white flowers down onto the roof all summer long.

Before I take my leave, Helen voices an important point concerning small gardens: 'Plants which only have a short flowering season and then look tatty and tired are impossible in a garden of this size; the mistakes and spent plants show because everything is so close. So my short-flowering permanent plants, camellias and bulbs for instance, are all in pots. Lilies, which I could not live without in June and July, look terribly depressing towards the end of the summer. But if they are in a pot that can be spirited away out of sight, while being fed for next year's flowers, something else can take their place.'

GOTHICK LINES

Opposite. *A weathered lead container sits well on old stone paving where its decoration quietly echoes that of the Victorian gothick cast-iron seat. The scheme of blue and violet flowers completes this restful garden corner. (p.142)*

SUSPENDED FLAMINGO

Opposite. *Surrounded by* Clematis *'Gravetye Beauty', a wall sconce sports the strange succulent growth of* Oenanthe japonica *'Flamingo', its pewter green leaves edged pink. During summer the trailing growths will cover the pot.*

PEACHY TREAT

Above. *New peachy colour forms of* Argyranthemum *and* Verbena *are used, not to disguise the rich tones of this slip-washed terracotta vase, but to enhance them. (p.142)*

BOXED ALLEY

Opposite. *Stark white-painted walls provide the ideal backdrop to these smart potted topiary shapes of box,* Buxus sempervirens. *This clever combination has transformed this formerly dark side passage into an elegant garden approach.*

CHICKEN AND EGG

Above. *In the corner window of the garden room green- and purple-leaved basil, planted in an amusing terracotta pot, thrive in the warmth and sunlight.*

CHATSWORTH
The biggest containers in the world

HER GRACE THE DUCHESS OF DEVONSHIRE

he sudden dramatic appearance of the west front of Chatsworth, revealed through venerable parkland trees, takes you by surprise. On crossing James Paine's classical eighteenth century bridge, the final approach to the house is made, at which point the awesome scale of the house becomes apparent.

The present Duke and Duchess of Devonshire have restored and contributed a great deal to the garden. Her Grace the Duchess of Devonshire told me, 'We didn't move in until 1959 and so there had been a long time with nothing at all happening in the garden. There was a school here all through the war when the lawns were not even mown.' She went on to mention some of their achievements in the last thirty years.

'We have added a lot since we've been here: that's to say we have planted the double pleached lime avenue on the south lawn, the serpentine hedge and the maze; and cleared out acres and acres of laurel and wild rhododendron in the two-mile pinetum walk which is nearly finished now. The kitchen garden is the latest project which has become a passion of mine.'

SPIRALLING HEIGHTS OF GRANDEUR

Opposite. *The approach to the Orangery is defined by a large pair of pots containing lemon trees. Either side of the ramp grow different cultivars of ivy trained on spiralling wires (p.143). In the background, Sir Joseph Paxton's great conservative wall, for peach growing, marches up the hill.*

The kitchen garden is an area of land just beneath the wooded hills which rise up behind the house, adjacent to the old stable yard and once used as an exercise paddock. Latterly this was a conventional vegetable garden, but over the past two years it has been transformed most dramatically. Radiating rows of vegetables are grown on west-facing raised beds looking out over the great grey roofs of James Paine's stable yard and beyond across Lancelot ('Capability') Brown's park. Vegetables such as the brilliant red rhubarb chard, purple-stemmed varieties of Brussels sprouts and rich purple leaves of the beetroot 'Bull's Blood' are all grown here, contained within lush edgings of succulent parsley and wild strawberries.

Large cast-iron cauldrons, once used for boiling up beans for animal fodder are now used as corner pieces to the raised beds, planted with cabbages and French beans. Chimney pots removed from their lofty positions on the house also spend their retirement years in the kitchen garden with pelargoniums and nasturtiums in fiery colours drifting from their tops.

The Duchess is rightly proud of her latest project and even of the new vegetable-garden compost heaps. 'When you see what they produce and how marvellous the compost is, especially now we know not to buy peat if possible. One of the compost bins is terribly glamorous because in the spring it is all camellia petals, and then it's all grape thinnings. It is so very decorative a compost heap.'

In what the Duchess called a shed but what

MAMMOTH POTS

Above. *These beautiful orchid pots bear the maker's mark of J. Mathews, Royal Pottery, Weston-super-Mare. The large pot measures twenty-four inches high by thirty-three inches in diameter. Full of orchids it must have been an awesome sight . . . but perhaps such pots belong to another era. Quietly resting here is a more dignified retirement than being manicured for display in a museum.*

transpired to be one side of a magnificent arch leading to the site of the conservatory, a locked door is opened by Jim Link, the head gardener at Chatsworth. In the gloom our eyes took a moment to adjust, Jim moved to one side; standing next to him were some huge terracotta orchid pots with rows of holes around the sides, the size of golf balls, where once orchids grew. The pots were almost certainly made for use in Joseph Paxton's great conservatory, which was completed in 1840 but sadly demolished in 1920.

There are but few terracotta containers at Chatsworth. The Duchess explains: 'This is really stone country, it has a hard northern look about it and, somehow, terracotta is wrong, I think.' But in the old stable yard very large Tuscan terracotta pots are used to hold orange and lemon trees around a fountain. Of this she comments, 'I think this area has a certain Italian look about it. You might well be in Rome, mightn't you? So I think it's fine here. But then our wooden tubs – the ones we make – ', she indicates some Chatsworth Carpenter's tubs planted with standard bay trees nearby, 'I think look fine anywhere.' These are a range of solidly built wooden boxes, some with cylindrical 'cotton reel' finials at their corners, produced in the workshops of the maintenance department on the Chatsworth estate where beautifully designed and constructed garden furniture is also built.

The Derbyshire climate of long cold winters with frost often well into the month of May and Chatworth's high exposed position, does mean that winter gardening is something of a challenge. Containers planted for display in winter are not attempted. As the Duchess says: 'The winter is a dead loss here. We could try perhaps, but I don't think we would succeed somehow, we are just too exposed. Cabbages would grow I suppose.'

For the summer planting in the garden the Duchess says: 'I have given up trying the complicated things which don't like the climate; I would far rather have plants that do well, how ever common they may be.' Though she did add, 'Every time I go to someone else's garden, I just give up and think, what are we not doing that they are? But you can't copy everything, you just have to do what is suitable. It is our scale here that has to be watched, it's so enormous that you can't spend too much time on very small details.'

On the south front of the house, bay trees grown in Chatsworth tubs ornament an impressive staircase which rises to the first floor entrance. Every turn of the stair has in its corner another standard clipped bay and, without the fussiness of flowers, they contribute greatly to the architecture of the flight. 'Don't you think one grows through all the flowers and colour and gets to the shapes?' But having said that the Duchess went on to tell me how she felt rather disheartened when twice during the previous year she had been stopped by visitors in the middle of the garden, on the lawn below the cascade, and asked, 'Excuse me could you tell me where the garden is?' She laughs, taking this in good spirit.

The bay trees are trimmed in July, a drop in the ocean compared with the rest of the annual hedge clipping. Yew, box, lime, beech and even tulip trees add up to an impressive surface length (each side of a hedge and its top) of nearly five miles or a surface area of 5.39 acres. Jim Link and his team face this daunting prospect in early July when clipping begins in the west garden. Here yew and box shapes are geometrically arranged within Sir Jeffrey Wyatville's architectural parterres.

These parterres are built of ornamented stone-work which raise the soil level by four-and-a-half foot within them and form what the Duchess calls 'the biggest containers in the world'. They were built in the early part of the last century for the sixth Duke. They are now planted very successfully with shapes of yew and box in green and gold, replacing annual bedding schemes of former times. The green and gold sharply clipped shapes give a strikingly bold planting, complimentary to the strong architectural lines of the raised parterre, which looks attractive right through the year.

Perhaps I have found some winter 'pots' at Chatsworth after all!

SERENE SIMPLICITY

Below. *Sir Jeffrey Wyatville's architectural parterres are all planted identically with yews and box. Here nature has been tamed by man (and woman); beyond is one man's conceived idea of wilderness in 'Capability' Brown's parkland.*

A LIVING STAIRCASE

Opposite. The mighty south front of Chatsworth looks out over the seahorse fountain on the south lawn, and beyond to the canal pond and Paxton's Emperor fountain. The impressive staircase rising to the first floor might appear unwelcoming in summer were it not for the standard bay trees which create a living hillside on the stone steps. The bays are planted in Chatsworth Carpenter's boxes, and their number dictates a muted green which blends into the stonework. A pale or showy colour would pin-point every one of the sixteen containers from a quarter of a mile away. The silvery rosettes of verbascums are set to take over where they can. (p.143)

IN JAMES PAINE'S STABLE YARD

Above. Within the rusticated walls of the stable block a central fountain plays above a raised pool. Stone paving covers the yard with gravel at the four corners. This is an elegant, architecturally strong and majestic composition, but should one garden in an area such as this? To plant climbing roses, clematis and honeysuckle up these fine walls would be vandalism equal to covering them with graffiti. Yet a little greenery does enhance the courtyard. It comes in the form of four standard lemon trees placed at the canted pool corners. Terracotta pots, planted with citrus fruits, can be used, as this area is divorced from every other at Chatsworth.

BRIMMING BOXES

Left. Beneath gold-leaf-covered window, a series of ten cast-iron boxes, textured and painted to resemble stone, furnish the ledges. Here, as everywhere at Chatsworth, the scale must be appropriate for the house, hence the seven-foot long boxes. They are planted with pelargoniums in two shades to give a cheerful lift to the great stone facade. (p.143)

A CAULDRON OF BEANS

Above. This is one of a pair of similarly planted cast-iron cauldrons placed at the corners of one of the raised beds in the kitchen garden. Unpainted, they merge into their surroundings, adding height but not dominance. Ironically they are planted with dwarf beans; in former times beans for animal fodder were boiled up in these same cauldrons. (p.143)

A WILTSHIRE MANOR HOUSE
Elegant perfumed ladies

MELANIE CHAMBERS

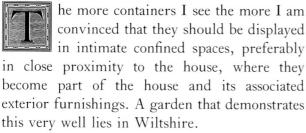

The more containers I see the more I am convinced that they should be displayed in intimate confined spaces, preferably in close proximity to the house, where they become part of the house and its associated exterior furnishings. A garden that demonstrates this very well lies in Wiltshire.

Here a series of closed areas around the house form walled and yew-hedged courtyards of great charm and individuality. Placed on the uneven stone paving are large fine containers of copper, stone and lead which blend with the very grey Wiltshire stonework of the paving and house walls. Within the paving borders have been formed for dianthus and low growing herbs and helianthemums. The containers contribute interest in proportion to the small area, while the house and hedges embrace them giving a feeling of security and shelter.

The present house dates from the early part of the seventeenth century, although a priory stood on the site in earlier times. The attractive walled divisions were added towards the end of the seventeenth century, including two pairs of sin-

SUNSHINE ON THE LEAD

Opposite. *An eighteenth-century lead cistern, weathered and aged after two centuries exposed to the English climate, plays host to a summer display of yellow and orange. Had such a show been planted in new terracotta or white-painted pot, the word brash might come to mind, but the old lead cools down the sunshine colours beautifully. (p.144)*

gle-roomed gate houses or garden gazebos. The walls, used together with early twentieth-century yew hedging, create a series of small gardens connected by a broad, yew-hedged walk which runs from the entrance court to a fine gate looking across the distant countryside.

The present owners have lived here for just six years, but they have been fortunate in engaging the help of Melanie Chambers. She describes herself as a peripatetic gardener; most would describe her as a freelance garden designer. Although working in many gardens, in Wiltshire, Gloucestershire and London, this one is home and rather special to her, as she has helped the owners since they first moved in. Together they are still refining the three-acre garden and rearranging what was there before.

We pause on our tour of the garden to look over the wooden kitchen-garden gates, beneath a listing walnut tree. Triangular plots are arranged around a circular stone-paved area where climbing roses and sweet peas clamber over wirework arches. We drink in the sweet apple aroma of the scented-leaved *Rosa eglanteria*, or sweet briar, which is clipped hard to form a low thorny hedge around some of the plots.

As we move on towards the house, past great empty olive jars too splendid to plant, we pause to look in 'Regent's Park'. This is a rectangular garden hedged with old yew on its longer sides and walls along the shorter. Why is it called 'Regent's Park'? Because before they were removed there were, within narrow grass paths, eight rectangular beds, each one filled with highly coloured large-flowered roses. The yew hedges are recovering from very drastic pruning. 'Regent's Park' has grown in width by eight foot in the last two years due to the removal of four foot of spreading yew hedge from each side. The bare yew trunks are now becoming covered by three-day stubble and in two or three years will be fully green again.

As we walk back to the courtyard, our conversation turns to containers. It is interesting to hear the opinion of one who uses them in so many different gardens: 'I often find that people are desperate to have colour around the house which is understandable, but it can ruin good architecture if plants are grown in borders in front of and over a house. Very often borders beneath a house cannot be seen from the windows, they are only enjoyed from the garden. But if containers are used then they can be placed just far enough away from the house to be viewed from indoors and from the garden. I am not very keen on flowers in a border against a wall opposite the windows of a house. I find this rather alien and contrived. I would much prefer to look at the wall with, say, two or three well-planted stone troughs placed against it.'

When planting up containers some golden rules are followed which make good sense: 'The key is not to stuff in as many different plants as you can around a major centre piece, it's just not necessary. Much better to use several specimens of the same plant to give impact and unity, then restrict yourself to three to four different plants within the container. The plants must be of a similar type. Too much of a *mélange* and the growth rates vary. Then you spend your life cutting some plants back to give room to others, especially as feeding to encourage the weaker plants can stimulate the stronger into undesirably vigorous growth.

The water requirements of a collection of plants within a container should also be similar. We have come to realize that fuchsias like to be kept a little drier than most other bedding plants; so we may create a planting of fuchsias and other plants which tolerate fairly dry conditions, like

FLORAL CENTREPIECE

Above. *A yew hedge topped with an amusing topiary rabbit gives seclusion to this small stone-flagged courtyard. Sunk into the centre is a millstone upon which rests a copper container of broad but low proportions, ideal for this situation. This is filled with seasonal bedding plants in spring and autumn. (p.144)*

Helichrysum, Aeonium, Artemisia, Echeveria or *Agave.*' To conserve water and to give weight and extra stability the tops of the containers are mulched with a thick layer of gravel. This also stops the new compost from flying everywhere when first watered, and keeps the roots cool.

We pass where previously a pair of *Heliotropium* 'Chatsworth' had stood either side of a sunny door. Now separated, these 'elegant perfumed ladies' were too hot, and have found shadier sites to stand in. We walk on to the glasshouse in only its second summer, massed with terracotta pots of

CHOCOLATE TROUGH

Above. *A fine old stone trough, mottled with lichen, is planted in strong deep tones. Salvias and pelargoniums support the centrally placed hot chocolate plant,* Cosmos atrosanguineus, *so-called for the distinctive scent of its rich velvety flowers which could deceive the* al fresco *diner into thinking that chocolate was to follow. (p.144)*

plants which spend some of their time inside the house and other times out recovering. There are some reconstituted-stone octagonal bowls planted with the large cranesbill, *Geranium palmatum*. Melanie enthuses, 'Don't they look wonderful? I brought them on in the glasshouse, put them out in April and this is their third flush of flowers this year.' The deeply lobed, dark green leaves fall down over the surface and sides of their containers forming a circular ruff over which showers of purplish red flowers are held on branched flower spikes.

Inside the glasshouse a ginger plant, *Zingiber spectabile*, has thrown up a seven-foot flowering spike of scarlet and yellow with intoxicating scent, causing great excitement. Equally spectacular and exotic yet nearly hardy in this country, *Melianthus major*, one of the most beautiful foliage plants, is grown here on its own in a large pot. The large glaucous leaves are jaggedly cut and the growth is luxuriant. Melanie cuts back old shoots and leaves to stimulate more lush foliage.

She then told me about a simple but dramatic planting she saw in the gardens of Villa Marlia near Lucca whilst on holiday. Atop a balustrade a row of twenty old terracotta pots were planted with alternate blue *Plumbago capensis* and brilliant red pelargoniums – it was a stunning sight which proved to her that a great variety of plant material is unnecessary.

I ask Melanie if she has container-grown plants of her own, or is she 'all gardened out' when she gets home? 'I have pots for all-year-round interest at home,' she says. 'A small terracotta basket pot with a box ball is outside my door. Inside, on a wide kitchen window ledge, I have an array of small old clay pots with myrtle and variegated box plants of different shapes and sizes. They stay in for most of the year, going out for the occasional rainy day to clean them up. I prefer shapes to flowers and colour. If I want colour I have spring bulbs – hyacinths and tulips – or, during the summer, lilies just on their own in pots. I prefer a simple unfussy look. Oh, but by my back door I do have a standard rose, 'Little White Pet', which is just beautiful and flowers for such a long time.'

This plant was surplus to requirements of one of the gardens so she has had the pleasure of its company this year. Beneath the rose she intended planting either the headily scented *Nicotiana suaveolens*, for a pure white composition, or perhaps some young *Heliotropium* 'Chatsworth', for a cool purple and white combination. 'I didn't get time to plant up the top of the pot. Perhaps I will next year if 'Little White Pet' hasn't found a new home by then!'

Gothick Daisy Box

Opposite. Argyranthemum foeniculaceum *grown in a sunny position naturally develops a rounded shape. Such a simple planting can also display an elaborate container to advantage. The gravel chippings help to conserve moisture.*

In a Quiet Corner

Above. *In the broad walk which connects the series of small gardens stands a pair of terracotta Ali Baba pots of ample figure, their lines untroubled by planting.*

ELTON HALL
A garden for 'The Empress'

MR AND MRS WILLIAM PROBY

I have to admit that every time the heavy iron garden gates clank shut behind me, and I crunch a few footsteps across the gravel path to be met by the extraordinary garden front of Elton Hall, I think of P G Woodhouse's Blanding's Castle. With its bizarre muddle of turrets, battlements and crenellations, Elton Hall could have been built as a 1930s Hollywood set to suit the over-indulgent imagination of a film director craving the eccentric English look. The house is, though, quite genuine. Although it is, as Mrs Proby says, 'a hodge-podge of different periods and styles', the earliest being the medieval tower of 1485 and a chapel of the same date some distance away. The two were to be linked by a succession of additions, firstly in the early part of the seventeenth century and then later in 1660 when the first Proby to live at Elton built on a Restoration house. Much has been added since then, right up to 1860 when a top floor, new wing and an impressive central tower were installed. 'I like it; it's a pleasing muddle. Perhaps I should have a pig like Lord Emsworth's "The Empress". Actually my daughter Alice would dearly love a pet pig,' said Mrs Proby.

William and Merry Proby came to live at the

SWAGGED SPHERE

Opposite. *A dwarf box ball is planted in a decorative stoneware pot. Although dwarf box is slow growing, it has the virtue of also being slow to fill a pot that common box would rapidly outgrow. (p.144)*

Hall in 1979 from a mews house in London. Both of their parents have been keen gardeners; William Proby's mother having always been interested in growing roses and Merry Proby's mother who just loved gardening. 'My mother used to do a lot of gardening, and I remember my father would prune quite radically. We children helped out at the odd times, cutting off the flower stems or bents which the lawn mower left behind. They used to pay us a penny a bent, but I was always more interested in ponies then.'

In London their house had no garden but it was in a broad cul-de-sac, so they had window boxes made for every window, and tubs and an enormous wooden trough, which looked like a giant coffin, under the front wall of the house. 'I used to go along to the local garden centre at Holland Park to buy bedding plants. In the "coffin" we had some shrubs, honeysuckle, roses and clematis as well as bedding. The house had, what the estate agent called a balcony which you could just about get your foot onto. We had a window box there full of bedding which looked pretty when the windows were open. So we made a garden out of nothing really.'

On arriving at Elton, Mr and Mrs Proby realized there was an enormous amount of renovation work which badly needed doing to the house, which meant that apart from grass cutting and tidying there was little time for the garden. Merry Proby now regrets this, 'When you move into a house I think you should look at the garden and, if necessary, make structural alterations in the first winter. It takes such a long time for hedges and trees to begin to look anything at all.'

The garden was 'a bit of a desert' when they arrived. Much had been removed to save on labour expenses, flower beds had disappeared, but, more tragically, ancient yew hedging, topiary and a maze had all been cleared. From 1985 a rebuilding programme has been underway, establishing yew and hornbeam hedges, replanting the rose garden, and creating new herbaceous borders and a shrubbery. A newly planted orchard and fresh pieces of topiary are now in place. A more recent project has been the sunken garden formed around a small formal pool and surrounded by L-shaped beds.

In the sunken garden stoneware pots have been planted with dwarf box balls to give greater importance to the three flights of stone steps which lead down to the central pond. 'They're wonderful pots. They are a little touch of Italy, too, which is rather nice.' Merry once lived in Italy for a short time, near Florence at a village called Impruneta where many of the fine pale Tuscan terracotta pots are made. 'The house where I stayed had a very simple terraced garden, large pots of clipped box, and orange and lemon trees arranged along each terrace in rows. The whole garden was surrounded by olive groves. It was very beautiful.'

At the foot of the house walls at Elton are to be found many large square boxes built of brick and finished with stucco marked to resemble stonework. These were constructed as part of the 1860 improvements, presumably as part of the Victorian obsession for clothing buildings with creepers to give a romantic appearance. Some of the plants still survive in the boxes, 'I have cut back a lot of the creepers because I prefer to be able to see the architecture of the house and the

ARCHITECTURAL EMBELLISHMENTS

Right. *As the flowers of summer recede with the onset of autumn, the potted evergreens come into focus. These emphasize architectural features in the garden, steps and entrances, much as the stone balls and sphinxes do for the house. (p.144)*

stonework. Near the front several of these boxes have creepers intact. There they are useful as the area is dark and cold, facing as it does north, where very few plants would thrive. Having said that, the green-and-white-variegated dogwood and the golden cut-leaved elder do well growing in these boxes where they give light and brightness to one of the darkest of corners. In winter these shrubs, including the creepers, lose their leaves so the austere look returns.'

When I ask Merry about colour in the garden she says, 'Oh I always instantly veer towards pinks, blues and creams; the safe traditional colours. I'm not averse to using yellows, oranges and reds, but I don't like them muddled in with the softer colours. We have used yellow and orange in the tubs around the stable yard. That's rather fun because they are bright and cheery, and in the stable yard the colours can be isolated. There is a definite divide between the yard and the garden around the house.'

Above the sunken garden a broad area of paving has recently been relaid incorporating a series of old mill stones. This west-facing raised platform is to become a new sitting-out area and an ornate wood trellis is planned for the high wall to the rear. The large pots intended to line this terrace are to be of terracotta, which I query against the pale stone walls. 'I think it is absolutely fine, so long as you use the very pale Italian terracotta. I like the pots from Impruneta, but so much terracotta is too red for this part of the world. I don't believe we could use *any* terracotta right against the house; this is just far enough away to get away with it. If I can find somewhere suitable to overwinter them, I intend planting the pots with orange and lemon trees, reminiscent of the terraces at Impruneta.'

Ivy Globes

Left. *A pair of large Versailles boxes stand either side of the front door, each planted with just one Hedera helix 'Glacier' trained over a wire globe. Few other evergreens would survive in such a cold dark position.*

A Global Failure?

Opposite. *A globe made from supple one-year-old growths of willow sits neatly onto its pot, the intended support for a decorative convolvulus.*

However, *although leafy basal growth was produced, neither twining stems nor flowers developed. Probably the compost was too rich. (p.144)*

Shady Variegation

Above. *The white-margined leaves and light airy form of this dogwood make it an excellent candidate for brightening a*

shady wall. Dogwoods tolerate a certain amount of shade, and in winter the young twigs of this species have red bark. (p.144)

WASHINGTON GARDENS
Bold foliage in Fredericksburg

PHILLIP WATSON

hillip Watson is an enthusiastic and imaginative garden designer from Fredericksburg, Virginia. I first met him at Rosemary Verey's garden, then again at the Chelsea Flower Show, 1992, where he was helping Rosemary with the garden she was building for the *Evening Standard*.

Phillip explained to me how, when on foreign studies in France, he made his greatest horticultural discovery: 'Rosemary Verey. She instilled in me an awareness of life's small treasures. "Seize the moment," she would exclaim, "be it shafts of late afternoon sun lighting the torch-like spires of the potted camassias or heavy dew sparkling like diamonds on a spider's web".'

This cherishing of the otherwise overlooked or taken-for-granted detail has stayed with Phillip, and is infused in his work.

A great enthusiasm and energy for gardens was tested to the full at Chelsea. He flew into Heathrow Airport from Washington, arriving early morning. Straight away Phillip travelled to the Royal Hospital showground in Chelsea for a full day's work on the garden exhibit; a day that saw temperatures high in the eighties. He then drove Rosemary back to her home in Gloucester-

SWIMMING-POOL SALVIAS

Opposite. *The tall spires of salvias add height to a poolside planting and, with the addition of pinks and mauves, an unrestrained medley results. The whole display is elevated above the surrounding border.* (p.145)

shire, and from where they motored back to London the following morning – early. He admitted to being tired!

Phillip is a born gardener and had plants potted from an early age. 'My first potted plant was a Shumard oak, grown from an acorn in my second-grade class. My second was a pot of spider lilies dug from my grandfather's garden, I admired their dark green winter foliage. From these experiences I learnt, early on, that pots weren't just for pelargoniums and begonias.'

Upon graduating from Mississippi State University with a degree in horticulture, Phillip pursued some foreign studies in Europe; first in Holland, then Scotland and France. He returned to America to take up work in Manhattan designing rooftop gardens. 'My interest in potted plants reached a crescendo while in New York. Everything was grown in containers, but their arrangement had to look like a conventional garden. Although I didn't use oaks, other trees of large stature were potted up. Rows of containerized yews became hedges, and groupings of potted annuals became flower beds. So re-doing the garden was much like re-arranging the living room.' After five years of being deprived the joy of having his own garden he moved to Fredericksburg.

Fredericksburg is fifty-five miles south of Washington DC. It was established in 1728 and saw much fierce fighting during both the War of Independence and Civil War. Some ancient catalpa trees which bore witness to these troubles still stand. Phillip's first reaction to what he saw

Cuphea Collection

Above. *Three* Cuphea hyssopifolia *trained up into miniature standard specimens flower all summer long. Beneath them grow strongly variegated arabis which clothes the surface of the pots, acting as a living mulch to conserve moisture. (p.145)*

in Fredericksburg was to look out his pruning shears. 'Boxwood seemed to have swallowed the historic district whole. What was once edging box, now resembled great storm clouds. Carefully I set out to tame the beast, but somewhere along the line the hunter was captured by the game. I don't use large amorphous boxwoods in my designs, but I still find them charming in a nostalgic sense.'

Virginia possesses a climate of extremes. Winters cold enough to kill camellias give beautiful winter tones to conifers. Summers sunny enough for nandinas to set heavy fruit cause drought. These extremes are not so great as to prevent an array of plants flourishing, almost unrivalled in any other region of America. Drought is overcome by the use of efficient irrigation equipment, and strong damaging winds that arrive with late summer storms are pre-empted by thorough staking of tall annual growth. In the more exuberant of pot plantings, extra weight for stability is given by using large stones and bricks as drainage material in the base of the pot.

To meet the needs of a clientele with ever-discriminating taste, Phillip now grows many rare and unusual plants in his own nursery. 'Currently I grow all my perennials and annuals, as well as a vast range of hard-to-find conifers and flowering shrubs. Most of these plants can be found in my display gardens around the property for client viewing.'

Phillip's assignments take him as far north as Connecticut and as far south as Key West, Florida. He also lectures, and now exhibits at the New York and Philadelphia Flower Shows, which as he says, 'Provide forums to showcase my latest design ideas.'

The gardens he has designed range widely in style, from the acutely formal to the outright 'raucous'. 'Both extremes, however, display degrees of humour reflecting the character of the client, or possess a character the client admires. It's a bit like playing matchmaker, so a love of the garden can develop.'

Phillip goes on to describe the gardens he creates: 'Vast selections of annuals and perennials are utilized in my gardens, usually enclosed within a framework of clipped evergreens, or punctuated with shaped conifers or hollies. A number of flowering shrubs such as buddlejas, vitex, and caryopteris are used liberally to attract butterflies. Open-canopied trees including honeylocust, redbud, and crab apple may be festooned with non-invasive climbers, like carefully selected cultivars of clematis and rose. Colour saturates the picture presenting a kaleidoscope of hues that changes with the seasons.'

As it is in Britain, terracotta is popular in America and Phillip uses it in a variety of locations in his own and clients' gardens. For extra impact he sometimes paints terracotta a crisp white, which has the curious effect of hardening the lines of a normally warm-textured object. When planting up he tends to use an assortment of plants within each container, and the individual pots of different shapes and sizes are grouped together in a selected location, often as a welcoming display by a front door.

Leaf colour and shape are given equal importance to flowers. Strong contrasts of light green and gold-leaved plants are used with the deepest rich purple foliage to create sunlight and shade even on overcast days. The collections of pots are colourfully planted, one could say with too much

A Pristine Painted Pot

Below. *A two-tiered planting dominated by a large Italian terracotta pot which, after receiving several coats of paint, has taken on a different personality. Once weathered its appearance may suffer, necessitating an annual 'touch-up'. (p.145)*

vibrancy of colour. But because of a carefully constructed theme which runs through each group of pots and often on into the surrounding shrub or herbaceous borders, Phillip manages to avoid the brash and the obvious.

Where he wants to draw attention to one particular container, he punctuates it with more colour to attract the eye in the same way that a red pillar box stands out in a crowded city street. Low trailing plants often lost at ground level are elevated to new heights in Phillip's gardens by planting them in containers placed upon pedestals situated within herbaceous borders, 'Serving to bring plants such as vinca and verbena to the top of the picture.'

The pots and other containers around Phillip's garden are not only well planted but, like the gardens themselves, they are very well maintained. On a visit to an English garden together one summer, he told me: 'Whether you're developing a miniature gardenscape in a container, or a full-size herbaceous border on a grand scale, attention to detail is essential. Many plantings are beautiful at a glance, but few improve on close inspection.' With this in mind all his containers are regularly preened: removing fading flowers to encourage a further flush of blooms, and yellowing leaves as the planting ages.

Phillip utilizes wall baskets and old hay racks. Lined with moss and heavily planted, they cascade flowers and foliage from the wall. These containers are particularly effective when planted with some of his bold foliaged plants and mounted on a brilliantly white-washed wall. They look like sculptural works of art.

Constantly thinking up new ideas, Phillip's latest experiments are in the creation of miniature bog gardens contained within stone troughs. He also plans to exploit the qualities of a wider range of dwarf conifers for use as accents in containers, and to use more broadleaved evergreens to provide structure and support for neighbouring annuals. The imaginative flow of ideas shows no sign of drying up and I look forward to seeing future developments – they are sure to be innovative.

PETRIFIED 'POT'

Opposite. Phillip has provided this book with its oldest container; a fossil log which at sixty-five million years old, makes eighteenth-century urns a mere blink of the eyelid in time. The hollowed centre of the short petrified log, protruding from beneath a dwarf conifer, is home to a shell pink antirrhinum. The surrounding border is extremely detailed with clever use of leaf colour and shape. Groundcover plants, so often thought of as uninteresting, here make a lively patchwork with thanks to lysimachia, thyme and variegated arabis. (pp. 145–6)

POOLSIDE PANACHE

Above. Carefully arranged on a swimming-pool terrace, these containers make a splendid summer show. The dramatic purple-foliaged plants contrast well with the fine golden leaves of acorus and lysimachia and flowers in shades of pink. A pot of ivy has been made into a basket-like structure, with its handle supported by wires, from which spill impatiens and golden origanum. Overall the well-spaced arrangement shows off the pots as a collection of individuals, but linked by a common theme. (p. 146)

IMPATIENS PERCH

Opposite. *Part of a garden arch accommodates a small strawberry pot with planting holes stuffed full of New Guinea* impatiens. At the foot Monarda 'Sunset' *and* Rudbeckia hirta *create a wash of colour, suitably bright for a Virginian summer.*

A PLACE TO SIT AND ADMIRE

Above. *Verbenas are the staple of many a gardener's container. They have ferny foliage, a long flowering season and stems which* *weave among other plants or spill down the sides of a solitary pot to link container to garden.* (pp. 146–7)

THE ROYAL BOTANIC GARDENS
Kew revisited

MIKE SINNOTT

My first look at the Royal Botanic Gardens, Kew, was in 1976. It must have been in July for there were foreign students playing under the water sprinklers trying to keep cool in what was to be one of the hottest summers of the century. The lawns had turned straw colour, and I remember great clumps of yuccas sporting flower spikes like ivory towers way above my head. They were certainly enjoying the heat, similar to their native southern United States. Little did I know then that four years later I would be paying another visit of a more permanent nature, enrolling as a student, setting sail on a three-year voyage of botanical and horticultural discoveries which were to help me through hereafter. It did, then, seem fitting that this great institution should play a part in my first few strokes across the deep waters of the literary world. I was thrilled when they accepted my approach for an interview.

Photographer Andrew Lawson and I slipped in with just a nod from the gardens' constabulary at 6.15 am one sparkling July morning with only squirrels and Canada geese to get in the way of the lens. The urns and vases, tubs and pots looked splendid. Their positioning is precise; like a well-timed punch line they give maximum impact.

Some weeks later I returned seeking the man responsible for the bedding schemes. Mike Sinnott is Assistant Curator of the Herbaceous Section which encompasses the Alpine House, Rock Garden and Woodland Garden; the family or order beds where related plants are grown together; the seventeenth-century period garden around Kew Palace; the herbaceous plantings in the Duke's garden and in the grass and aquatic gardens; the bedding schemes running down the sides of the Broad Walk; and the parterre in front of the Palm House.

Formalities were soon dispensed with after common ground had been quickly recognized not just with familiar plants, but with another 'plant', some would say a pernicious weed, which has always run riot at Kew. Going by the name of *Vitis kewensis*, commonly called the Kew grapevine, it bears the fruits and seeds of gossip as freely, it seems, as when I was a student.

Our conversation turned to Mike's predecessor who was Assistant Curator of this section in my student days. 'Brian Halliwell brought an element of the unusual and experimental into what had been solely floral "parks department" style bedding displays,' Mike Sinnott explained. 'He contributed a lot to what are grown as bedding and container plants today in this country, particularly in terms of the tender perennials now so popular. He brought these plants to the attention of commerce and to the general public through displays here at Kew and

A CENTRAL FEATURE

Opposite. *Early morning sun illuminates the fine detailed vase which stands high above massed* Pelargonium *Multibloom Salmon, punctuated in places by* Melianthus major. *Tall* Lavatera *'Barnsley' help to break the severe square lines of the urn's plinth.*

by exhibiting plants with potential at Royal Horticultural Society shows in Westminster. Plants that had been forgotten or never used widely in horticulture were introduced to a much wider audience. Not all of them worked, some were just not suited to ornamental display. It was trial and error but the important thing was that he was adventurous. I hope it can be said that we are carrying on in a similar vein.'

While talking we have been approaching a large unplanted urn surrounded by a round border which acts as a roundabout at the Palm House end of the Broad Walk. 'I would like to see this urn planted, but its plinth is unstable and needs repair. Personally I would like the plinth reduced in height as it is overbearing in this position. To try to counter this we have planted *Lavatera* 'Barnsley' to mask its base. Unfortunately the heavy rain this summer seems to have made them very leafy with very little flower apart from an early flush in June.'

Indicating a border with some specimens of *Melianthus major* Mike comments, 'These are good structural plants. We have used them here as dot plants through pink pelargoniums. Unfortunately the melianthus contracted a bad infestation of blackfly early in the season. As we have a minimum spray policy at Kew we only take action when the insects prove a serious threat to the life of the plant, so the plants suffered a serious check which is why they are still on the small side.' The melianthus are propagated at Kew in the micropropagation unit which produces plants by tissue culture. This method has the advantage of producing identical plants, ideal when using thirty dot plants together.

The border is edged with a small neat silverfoliaged *Tanacetum densum amani*, traditionally grown as a scree plant on the rock garden. 'Next year this is due to be used in the Palm House parterre. We need 4,400 plants next spring and these will provide the cuttings. We cannot afford to keep a nursery stock ground so we have to be rather cunning using the smaller borders in the Broad Walk to increase a limited amount of bedded-out stock which at the end of the summer

will provide enough cuttings or divisions for the containers and larger displays the following summer. It's a very economical way of reproducing plant material.'

To be a star in one of the large containers or main bedding schemes is a very demanding role, and Mike will have often grow his plant combinations together a year in advance to check heights and colour tones. The flower colour obviously has to be correct but the plant must also flower freely throughout the summer months. It should be drought tolerant, of strong constitution so not requiring staking, rain tolerant to avoid flowers and flower-buds spoiling and, if possible self-cleaning (dead flower heads detaching from the plant and falling to the ground). These are tall orders, but many of Mike Sinnott's plants do comply. They have to these days! 'We have limited means to deadhead everywhere now, so many plants have to be self-maintaining as far as is possible.'

We have now reached the magnificent Palm House designed by Decimus Burton and erected between 1844 and 1848, its graceful lines make it one of the most beautiful of greenhouses, like an elegant bird cage. In front lies the extensive Victorian-style parterre and the Pond, edged by a parapet punctuated by tazzas filled with yellow and blue bedding to compliment the parterre.

Mike was interested to discover which of several blue daisy flowers would perform best in the tazzas. 'These are *Felicia amelloides* 'Read's Blue', they have grown and flowered a little but not enough. *Felicia gracilis* flowered early on and then not at all for months. *Brachycombe multifida* flowered very well early on, then it seemed to run out of steam and didn't grow any more after

FIERY POMEGRANATE

Opposite. *A simple oak whisky barrel placed in a sheltered corner of the Queen's Garden plays host to a burgeoning dwarf pomegranate,* Punica granatum *'Nana'. The long flowering period and attractive small glossy leaves makes this tender shrub an interesting specimen.*

CLASSICAL ORNAMENTS

Above. *A pair of arc-shaped borders flank the path leading to the Aroid House, near the Main Gates. Victorian-style bedding uses* Canna 'Assault', Agryranthemum foeniculaceum *and, to give a dark edging, the foliage plant* Iresine lindenii.

SUPPORTED BY DOLPHINS

Left. *One of a pair of beautifully simple vases each held aloft by four acrobatic dolphins. Despite recent repair work, they are too fragile to bear the weight of compost, so are left unplanted. Their soft creamy colouring links them effortlessly with the classical Aroid House in the background.*

midsummer. *Felicia amelloides* 'Santa Anita' is the only one we shall use extensively in the future. It grows well, flowering over a long period and its outer petals or sterile florets are half as long again as the species.

'A small yellow daisy with a dark eye called *Sanvitalia procumbens* has been on trial too. This North American native won a bedding-plant-of-the-year award three years ago in America.' It has grown and flowered well on the parterre, but in the urns it looks like it requires a little more water and liquid feed to allow it to fill out, as do *Heliotropium* 'Chatsworth' which appear to need a lot of water.

These urn plantings are at risk from visitors sitting on them or taking cuttings, as they are at a vulnerable height. Seagulls and other birds are also a problem as they enjoy sitting on the urns and disturbing the plants.

We walk down the Broad Walk passing on our right one of Kew's original garden buildings, the Orangery. A magnificently confident building designed by Sir William Chambers (who was also responsible for the Pagoda), it was built in 1761 for Princess Augusta, Dowager Princess of Wales and mother of George III, who lived at Kew House, also known as the White House (now demolished), just a short distance away. It is to Princess Augusta that the founding of Kew as a botanical garden can be attributed.

In front of us stands a fine pale vase, in and around which is a well co-ordinated planting. A splendid specimen of black-leaved *Aeonium* forms a pyramid of rosettes in the urn, interwoven by silver *Artemisia* and *Plectostachys*. Beneath, the circular bed is filled with concentric circles of the silvers, blues and purples of ornamental kales, cabbages and beetroot. All of these are individually pot-grown then planted out in May. 'You can see that we cheated with the aeoniums by planting a ring of single rosette plants around the edge of the vase. The artemisia is an excellent cultivar, *A. arborescens* 'Porquerolles', brought back by John Simmons, our Curator, from a visit to the botanical garden on the island of Porqueroll. Like the species, it is not reliably hardy.' Mike is

obviously and justly pleased with this planting. 'Not bad, not bad,' he says, as we make our way towards the main gate.

On our left another fine building, the Aroid House. This elegant Bath-stone glasshouse was one of four designed by John Nash and originally stood in the grounds of Buckingham Palace, where its fellows still stand. In 1836 it was brought stone by stone and re-erected at Kew. The path leading to the Aroid House is flanked by a pair of crescent borders planted with *Argyranthemum foeniculaceum*, *Iresine lindenii* and a flamboyant canna.

Placed within these borders are two pairs of vases each supported by three dolphins. These were planted up until a few years ago when they were found to be splitting. Repair work was undertaken and it was advised that they were still fragile and should not be replanted. Personally, I rather like them empty.

Back in Mike's office I ask what policy governs the ornamental areas of Kew – is it historical, botanical or purely decorative? 'The over-ruling factor is public display, so even when we play around with exotic or unusual plants we have to be sure they are going to provide colour through the season. The general public enjoy the very colourful schemes which I might describe as 'shockers'. Sometimes we tie a display scheme in with an event at Kew. In 1994 there is a conference here on the Compositae, the daisy family, so daisy plants will be dominant in the Palm House parterre.'

As for winter planting of containers, Mike says, 'We tried planting the urns in front of the Palm House with spring bedding and bulbs, but due to bird damage, waterlogging and frost damage this proved unsuccessful. It is very cold down there and the containers can freeze absolutely solid for days giving very patchy results in spring. The vase with the black *Aeonium* was planted last year with *Melianthus major*. It looked well through the summer and we left it in the urn all winter in the hope that it might do something, but it didn't. It got thoroughly frosted and sat there like a fossil!'

BLACK AND BLUE

Opposite. *The black rosettes of a tree-like aeonium dominate the vase to form a glistening pyramid beneath which artemisia and plectostachys weave and drape. Around the plinth, the* theme continues with decorative vegetables arranged in concentric circles. The colour tones of this display are magnificent; the scale of the planting perfectly balanced. (p.147)

PALM HOUSE BLUES . . . AND YELLOWS

Above. *Within the glare of Kew's most famous glasshouse, a series of tazzas decorate the parapet by the pond. The plants, which include* Sanvitalia procumbens *with its dark-* centred daisies and heliotrope, are carefully chosen to reflect colours used in the bedding scheme of the great Palm House parterre, visible in the background. (p.147)

COTSWOLD SECLUSION
Sinuous urns

MR AND MRS SMITH

erched on the side of a valley, on the
northern edge of the Cotswolds, there
stands a manor house surrounded by
wooded hilltops. The position is open and
exposed to strong winds but the west-facing
garden is a delight to be in on a warm evening,
as it captures every last ray of sun till dusk.

The house and tithe barn, close by, bear date
stones to 1628. The magnificent barn remains
little altered, its great buttresses, like sturdy legs,
holding it in position. The house has been altered
upon two occasions. Firstly in 1846 by the
architect R C Carpenter, a follower of Augustus
Pugin, who enlarged the house and created
formal Victorian terraces from the sloping hillside to the north of the house. In 1935 the Arts
and Crafts architect Norman Jewson built a range
of rooms creating a new south front to the house.
He also built a walled garden onto this south end
of the house, incorporating a gabled gazebo into
one of the wall corners. This gazebo is reminiscent of Gertrude Jekyll's thunder house at Munstead Wood, Surrey, where she would look out on
stormy nights at the lightening over Godalming.
Jewson also undertook further terracing of the
hillside site to the south.

NYMPHS AND SATYRS

Opposite. *Fine details on a lead vase depict
alternate nymphs and satyr masks, and exuberant
acanthus leaves. With age, lead, like stone, grows
in beauty. Oxidation and a patina of algae and
lime builds up slowly to give an antique finish.*

Today the late-Victorian formal planting patterns have gone, and some of the 1930s paving
and pools have now disappeared. The terracing,
walls and steps that remain still form a strong,
structural backbone to the garden. The changes in
level are used advantageously, marked by containers. A row of beacon-like reconstituted-stone
urns surmount an eight-foot high retaining wall.
When seen from below the effect of the urns is
one of lightening and relieving the imposing slab
of wall. Viewed from the upper terrace level, the
urns sit at chest height close enough for their
contents to be examined and to appreciate them as
garden embellishments. Their planting is colourfully strong, using pinks, purples and maroons,
which catches the eye from a distance and links
easily with a pair of rich purple *Cotinus coggygria*
'Foliis Purpureis' growing nearby.

A pair of stepped piers are decorated with fine
lead urns dripping with blue-flowered tender
summer bedding. As Mr Smith says, 'It's extraordinary how something slightly sinuous like an
urn has a tremendously softening effect on this
rather austere architecture of Norman Jewson.
Somehow you have a wonderful combination: a
pretty pot in itself and its ability to join the flower
beds with the rest of the garden. I think the urns
have a lovely effect in the garden and we should
have more really. I love them.'

On the old Victorian terraces, to the north of
the house, a new garden has been planted.
Coinciding with the new plantings, square stone
terraces have been created in the form of rectangular platforms from which to view the park.

Against the back walls of these terraces large lead cisterns have been placed. Filled with compost and planted with blue-flowered tender summer plants, they compliment the pink-, blue- and palest yellow-flowered herbaceous plants flourishing in the mixed borders either side of the terraces. Blue flowers are particularly well set off by Cotswold stone and, in combination with silver-foliaged plants, they pleasantly enhance the colour of lead.

The great rose expert and former National Trust gardens' consultant, Graham Thomas, advised on new plantings in the garden from 1976-86, a period which saw many changes to the garden and from which many benefits are still being reaped. One addition from this period was the planting of a short avenue of *Sorbus aria* 'Lutescens', the very silver-leaved whitebeam, along the southerly entrance to the house forecourt. These trees have now matured into a corridor of silver through which one drives, emerging at the house. This effect has been mirrored on the north terrace at the far side of the house with a second avenue leading into the garden. The whitebeams are mimicked in colour and shape by a different species, the silver leaved upright pear, *Pyrus nivalis*. These are planted in pairs either side of the stone viewing platforms, framing the lead cisterns; the silver-grey leaves of the pears perform an act of unification between stonework, borders and containers.

The many random pots of herbs usually clustered around the back door of the house have been replaced this year by an elongated raised bed. Built with stone retaining walls to sides and front and a west-facing high wall behind, it measures twenty foot long but only eighteen inches wide. Here many herbs will be grown in good warm, free-draining conditions, much better suited to herb cultivation than the area formerly used, a north-east facing spot, dark and damp in winter which was conducive only to poor etiolated growth and regular deaths. Now the owners can look forward to a year-round, inexhaustible supply of fresh herbs from an attractively arranged raised bed, or container – of sorts.

CISTERN SETTING

Opposite. Set on stone paving, against the terrace retaining wall, a large container such as this makes a strong contribution to a garden scheme. In such a generous volume of compost, plants grow well, with lots of leafy growth. (pp.147–8)

SEVENTEEN-NINETY-SEVEN

Above. A detail from one of a pair of lead cisterns with fielded borders cast in relief. The colour and texture of lead creates the perfect foil for plants with silvery foliage which trail becomingly down the sides of such a tall container.

JEWSON'S SOUTH FRONT

Right. *Verbenas, fuchsias and diascias in rich colours fill the weathered urns ranged along the upper terrace retaining wall. The strong colours are important to be visible from a distance. In late summer when most shrubs and herbaceous plants have ceased to flower, returning the garden to amorphous greens, these vases 'soldier on', flowering until the first frosts cut them down in October. (p.148)*

COPPER GENTIANS

Above. *A copper filled with lime-free compost supports a thriving colony of* Gentiana sino-ornata. *The garden soil is far too alkaline to grow such plants, and would only result in their sure decline and death. By using a container the ideal conditions can be provided. Rainwater is used for watering as mains water is likely to contain lime which, eventually, would turn the acid compost alkaline.*

SUNNYSIDE FARM
Views from the gazebo

JIM KEELING

The tables were rather curiously turned the day I went to call upon Jim Keeling at Whichford Pottery. It was almost exactly three years previously, that he arrived tape recorder in hand to ask me my thoughts on pots, for his book *The Terracotta Gardener*, and now here was I doing the same. We settled ourselves within his gazebo overlooking the burgeoning walled garden planned and planted by Jim and myself four years ago.

Jim points out that before we begin, I should own up to planting his pots which are used at shows throughout the summer but are primarily planted for the Chelsea Flower Show in late May. Jim loves colour. So this year we abandoned restrained pastel shades and became much more adventurous using stronger, brighter colours together. As Jim says, 'This helped the new pots we were showing as it toned down the brightness of new terracotta which some people dislike. At the flower shows we attend, we like to be able to meet this criticism head on by using plant pots of different ages to demonstrate the evolution of a pot's surface.'

I have seen Jim, many times, scrutinizing an ageing pot held five inches from the end of his nose. Studying the developing patina of lime scale, algae and slight giving-off of clay salts, enthusing at its beauty, like an art historian marvelling at the many processes an old master has employed. 'I enjoy the obvious mortality of pottery. I have even grown to like the fact that it chips easily. I like the feeling of a very old pot that is almost at the end of its life; it is at its most beautiful then.'

Jim's interest in pottery came early when still a schoolboy. After University he realized that working in an office was not what he was cut out for. He wanted to use his hands in a creative job. Although he was keen to work on fine tableware pottery, he was given the sound advice firstly to become proficient at using a wheel for throwing all types of pots. He took a job for six months at a pottery near his parents' home in Surrey which happened to produce nothing but flower pots. On his last day Jim made 720 four-inch pots, averaging three per minute (a very experienced thrower could average five per minute, and so throw 1,200 pots per day). He had come to enjoy the challenge of working within commercial production constraints, and also liked the freedom of working with the less critically precise horticultural ware.

So Jim began setting up his own pottery, producing English terracotta garden pots of traditional shape and design. Gradually he began introducing larger and more elaborately decorated pots. Pots that would not be banished to the cold frame or greenhouse, but could grace the most elegant town house garden or country house

IN THE PINK

Opposite. *By later summer, a planting such as this fuses together, blending flowers and foliage into a spectacular display. The Ali Baba jar is not filled with compost, but has a small pot, fully planted, lodged in its neck. (p.148)*

terrace. Nowadays a large team is employed for the many processes involved in the manufacture of flowerpots, from Richard who refines the raw clays to Jane who organizes national advertising for the next regional sales. Jim is interested in the fact that the quality of the finished product relies entirely upon the level of skill, competence and dedication of each individual involved in every process, not just in the throwers' skill. The pot throwers are rather like actors, they need good raw materials and a good 'production company' to support and project their talents.

The increased production at the pottery inevitably carries with it a degree of repetition and, even in this creative profession, monotony. Jim finds a release for some of his more artistic qualities in the garden. 'I like the more sculptural side of gardening so my natural inclination would be to just have green shapes. I like colour but I'm not so good at using it.' The colourful flower garden we are sitting in has a twin which almost acts as a negative image. In this other garden only insignificant small white- or green-flowered plants are grown. The emphasis is on dark green foliaged shapes and textures. Jim likes the simplicity of single plantings of green foliage in pots. 'The pots of hostas and ferns grouped by my back door look marvellous. They like it there, as it faces east and is shady.'

There are many clipped box shapes in pots which I know are given some special treatment, and I ask Jim about one in particular. 'Ah yes, my little rhomboid! It did start out in life as a cube but someone dropped a board on it, so it became diamond-shaped. It's only eight inches across and has been that size for ten years. I clip it twice a year. Alternate autumns, when the rootball is dry, I take it from its pot, knock a lot of the compost off and cut back some of its roots. Then I pot it up using fresh compost but the same small terracotta box it came out of. In effect I'm bonsaiing it, allowing it just enough growth to clip and look green and tidy. I love it because it always looks good whatever the season.'

I ask about the potted figs which spend the winter in a greenhouse and the summer on brick paving beside the greenhouse door. They seem rather big plants in quite small pots. 'It's good to keep the roots restricted as it encourages them to fruit, but these sixteen-inch pots are really too small now. Next spring I intend moving them up into twenty-inch pots. They fruit very well, but the watering of them, especially when the fruit is filling out, becomes very demanding. They really need watering two or three times a day.'

A project which has caught Jim's eye as we have been sitting talking in the shade of the gazebo, watching gnats dance over the still water of the 'Persian' pool, is a large bog-garden pot. He intends planting this as a focal point opposite to where we sit. It is against the north wall of the walled garden, so will stay cool and damp even in high summer.

A terracotta mask is already in position to drip water into the forty-inch wall pot. 'This pot will be filled with good heavy loam topped with pieces of that very absorbent rock, tufa, and then planted with ferns, primulas and other moisture-loving plants. I like the idea of a damp and dank area which can just be glimpsed rising above Solomon's seal, toad lilies and more ferns, with the creeping mind-you-own-business plant, *Soleirolia*, at its foot.

'I do have an idea for next year. I want to grow an avenue of gigantic ten-foot high yew trees, clip them into spirals or corkscrews and put them in very large pots down the drive to the pottery. Their simple dark lines would be in pleasing contrast to the brilliance of the summer pots. They would look fantastic! We must get started before winter, Rupert, otherwise another year will have slipped past.'

RED-BLOODED DISPLAY

Opposite. *In the midst of a jumble of weathered flowerpots, stands an orderly combination of red-flowered plants.* Pelargonium *'Crimson Unique' and* Verbena *'Lawrence Johnson' have fused together to create a dramatic composition in blood red. (p.148)*

SUSPENDED COLORATION

Opposite. *The power of constant liquid feeding is clearly demonstrated here: without it a wall pot of such modest dimensions could not support such a healthy display. (p.149)*

FOR SUMMER AND WINTER

Above. *A pot planted for winter virtue stands proud in a summer border. Centre stage is a standard variegated privet, up which spirals ivy to furnish the bare trunk. Another small-leaved ivy covers the compost. (p.148)*

PURPLE PATCH

Opposite. Very strong colours have been used together, to the exclusion of softer tones which would dilute the impact of the rich violet, purple and red flowers. At the rear of the picture, red orach and Lychnis coronaria *make a dazzling display. Both plants are more often found in the herb garden or herbaceous border, but they thrive in pots nonetheless. Fuchsia 'Violet Gem' is in a pot on its own as it prefers to be kept a little drier than the other plants. (p.149)*

A BASKET OF BRACHYCOME

Above. A mingling of two plants with flowers of similar size provides an attractive combination of blue and pink. To achieve equal proportions, plants of similar vigour must be used. Here the creeping growth of a diascia threads through the feathery foliage of Brachycome multifida. *These small, fine-rooted plants required only a shallow depth of compost in which to grow, so are ideally suited to a half-pot or pan. A purple-leaved sage completes the composition giving weight and good colour to the arrangement. (p.149)*

THE HALL AND THE VICARAGE
Surviving Crystal Palace

MYLES HILDYARD AND ISABELLA HILDYARD

These two neighbouring houses in Nott-inghamshire, belonging to the same family, provide a wonderful example of the versatility of container gardening. But firstly, I must explain the two quite different settings in which the containers are used. One is a large stone house, today of nineteenth-century appearance, which has undergone several metamorphoses from original medieval manor house, through Jacobean alterations to late eighteenth-century classic Georgian mansion, to its present form, a Hall in highly decorative Victorian-Italianate taste. The other is a simple elegant late-Georgian former vicarage built from sober red brick. The clean cut and lack of ornament makes a stark contrast to the Hall next door.

In 1853 the south front of the Hall was faced in stone, a new conservatory begun and a balustrade-edged terrace added. This balustrade was designed to be ornamented with a collection of urns. Mr Myles Hildyard, whose great grandfather instigated these alterations, told me, 'The urns along the front date from about 1853, many of them were missing or broken when I came to live here. From photographs taken in about 1880 we could see how many there once had been. To make up the numbers I bought some reconstituted-stone copies as close to the pale terracotta originals as possible and really, when the plants have grown over, you can't tell the difference.' These vase-like urns add great style to the front of the house, planted uniformly with the bright pink *Pelargonium* 'Ville de Paris' and trailing blue lobelia. In winter the urns are emptied of compost and stood down on the terrace behind the balustrade as the elevated position does not only ensure fine views, but strong winds, too, which have been known to blow the urns over.

The magnificent conservatory is architecturally incorporated into the end of the Hall, its arched glazed gable and curved roof take direct influence from Joseph Paxton's Crystal Palace. Plants from temperate regions still flourish here today. An adequate winter temperature is maintained by using the old hot-water pipe system beneath iron gratings in the floor. Exotics like bananas and bougainvilleas are longed for, but maintaining high enough temperatures for these would be like trying to fill permanently a hot air balloon as the structure measures twenty-two foot wide by forty-seven foot deep and forty foot high. The conservatory had been designed for growing palms, but their lofty canopies and bare trunks were not thought decorative enough and, coupled with the fact that they were threatening to break through the roof, they were carefully removed.

Entering the conservatory today a large pair of boxes flank the door. Originally for growing oranges, they now contain large specimens of *Camellia* which in midsummer resembled fine

CAST IN IRON

Opposite. Pelargoniums spill from a black-painted, nineteenth-century urn. It is often a problem to know what colour cast iron should be painted, but black with a distressing grey wash applied to the high points works well. (p.149)

glossy leaved laurels. I push on past giant fronds of tree fern, ready to shower the unsuspecting visitor with spores, on past huge trumpets of datura and small trees of bell-hung abutilon. But these are dwarfed by a towering mimosa, *Acacia dealbata*, which provides a fine canopy over all. A tall white marble fountain towards the back of the conservatory has a lower pool encircled by sweet smelling ginger plants in terracotta pots. The north-facing side wall is now draped with high climbing jasmine growing from a trough. In former times nothing was grown here as, unlike other parts of the conservatory, there was no planting bed. High above my head, suspended from the roof, the most ornate wirework hanging baskets gently swing, now unplanted and pristine having just returned from the hanging-basket hospital where they were repaired and restored as new. The baskets, some measuring four foot across, were originally displayed in the Crystal Palace. They look very much at home here, if a little forlorn without plants.

A short walk to the old vinery, contained within the rose clad, high brick wall of the kitchen garden, reveals a mass of colour, like a well-stocked artist's palette. For here, banked up on staging in different sized pots, a waterfall of pelargoniums empties itself before me. Old terracotta flower pots are used *en masse*, creating what must be a watering nightmare.

Across the churchyard at The Old Vicarage, large pots have completely transformed the back of the house from a car park to a courtyard. Kitchen windows look out across this area onto the riotous flowers and growth emanating from the terracotta pots. One pair of pots are planted purely decoratively with an explosion of colour while a second pair are planted with a useful mixture of herbs for the kitchen and, for fun, ornamental cabbages and nasturtiums.

Mrs Isabella Hildyard recalls containers she saw in South Africa when she was young: 'We grew hydrangeas in large wooden half-barrels placed under oak trees. It was a sight typical of many Cape farms and looked so peaceful. It's something I have longed to do here but there are no strategically placed oaks around.' She goes on to give me some other of her views on container planting: 'I am very impatient, I like a garden to happen fast. So while I am waiting twenty years for a yew hedge to grow, it's nice to know that in three months I can see a pot planting reach maturity. The garden at The Old Vicarage is still young, still evolving. Beds of shrubs and shrub roses are only at junior level, and herbaceous borders still of indeterminate undifferentiated plants. The "instant" pots are much appreciated.'

She talks about the pots around the house and their plantings, 'I hate angry colours like reds and yellows, although I am prepared to have the odd nasturtium in the vegetable pots which should be brightened up. With the terracotta pots and the old brick of the house, the pink, mauve and silver colour scheme that we use is just right. I do like the plants to be big enough, so that they really fill the pots and look dramatic.

'My vegetable and herb pots I love because I long for a potager, the pots are my pathetic attempt at a substitute. In fact, I think in a potager you should have pots with standard fruit trees and vegetables spilling out of them at the ends of walks.' Having always wanted containers of vegetables and herbs, she finally made them after seeing some very fine examples in Florida.

Mrs Hildyard finishes on a very succinct point: 'Often by late August gardens are pretty well beyond their peak. By September a garden can be really rather depressing, much of its beauty is so ephemeral. All the roses are gone, and somehow there is this feeling of everyone champing at the bit to chop at their gardens and clean everything up to plant their spring bedding; but pots just go on and on well into October.'

BENEATH THE FOUNTAIN

Opposite. *The conservatory fountain pool is ringed with old terracotta pots bursting with ginger lilies,* Hedychium gardnerianum. *They jostle for position with* Howea forsteriana *and* Strelitzia, *whose paddle-shaped leaves stretch out like arms towards the sun.*

ORNAMENTAL SPLENDOUR

Right. *The Victorian-Italianate front of the Hall is dominated at one end by the great curved roof of the conservatory. Along the terrace balustrade stand sixteen urns, used in places to emphasize flights of steps, linking house to garden.*

TRADITIONAL ORANGE BOX

Above. *Now home to a camellia, this box is an example of those used for the cultivation of citrus during the eighteenth century. It has removable sides, held in place by iron latches, to facilitate root pruning and replenishing the rootball with fresh compost.*

POTTED POTAGER

Opposite. *A terracotta pot of modest decoration is filled with an assortment of herbs, flowers and ornamental vegetables. Seen here in early autumn, the planting breaks all the traditional rules for combining colours and forms to achieve a balanced composition. Yet the* result is lively and amusing, *with intense pink and orange working together. The pot was planted to supply just a sprig of the many herbs needed in the kitchen. Nasturtiums add colour not only to the display but also to salads, for their flowers are edible. (p.150)*

CLASSICAL LINE-UP

Above. *The campana urns, positioned along the top of the balustrade, look out across the garden. In summer the urns are planted identically using the floriferous pink* Pelargonium *'Ville de Paris', now more correctly known by the less romantic-sounding cultivar name* of 'Henderinum', *and pale blue lobelias. To the west, stately cedars of Lebanon fringe the lawn, but directly to the south no protection is offered. This necessitates the removal of the urns to sheltered safety behind the balustrade for winter. (p.150)*

WHITE BARN HOUSE
A broad palette

BETH CHATTO

When I visited Beth Chatto one unseasonably damp day in July, I found her tremendous enthusiasm for plants and, in particular, her excitement at the creation of three newly planted areas almost eclipsed our talk of pots and pot plantings. In the previous year a further two acres have been added to the extensively planted three-and-a-half acres. A new dry garden has been made using plants capable of withstanding drought conditions for long periods of time. The whole area is mulched with gravel to conserve what moisture is present. Two new woodland gardens have also been created. One has a woodland floor of shade-loving herbaceous plants mulched with bark. The second has a tree canopy thin enough to allow a grassy sward to develop where flowering bulbs are massed from winter through to midsummer.

Her garden at Elmstead Market near Colchester was begun in 1960, on land covered by undergrowth and scrub. Clearing revealed a shallow valley and spring-fed ditch; unusual features for Essex. After shelter belts of trees were established and the ditch transformed into a series of pools, the planting began. At the same time a house of sympathetic lines was placed to one side of the shallow valley to utilize the fall of the land, splitting the house into two levels which relate to paved terraces outside. It is here where many and varied groups of pots are placed to be enjoyed on hot days from the terrace or from the large sitting-room windows.

'I first saw groups of pots arranged like this when peering through small iron-gridded gate windows into paved courtyards in France; they gave such colour and life to the area,' Beth recalls. She now practices the same principles for her own pots, using massed groupings with a single plant type in each pot. By late summer the whole will have grown together to form a 'potted border'.

During the winter emptied pots remain on the terraces, for Beth enjoys their different shapes grouped together. She adds, 'It is also practical because they don't have wet compost to freeze within them and possibly cause them damage. It also makes sure we remember to put in fresh compost every year.'

I admired some fine specimens of the large silvery blue and yellow striped rosettes of *Agave americana* 'Variegata' strategically placed on the terrace steps. Beth commented, 'You can't put an agave in a narrow-necked Ali Baba pot without destroying the agave or the pot. Their containers must be straight sided or flared outwards towards the top to enable the rootball to be removed easily. That is the reason why the agaves here are in black plastic pots, they are still to be grown on into larger plants in bigger containers.'

Beth enjoys foliage in a container as much as flowers: 'The marvellous contrast of big bold leaf

A SUMMER BLIZZARD

Opposite. *A corner of the sunny sitting-out terrace has pots grouped closely together. The small white button-like flowers belong to* Argyranthemum 'Blizzard', *but warmth is at hand in the form of pelargoniums, so vibrant in colour. (p.150)*

shapes like agaves, phormiums, cordylines', she enthuses, 'are *so* good. The combination of succulents to give different textures of leaf as well as leaf shape is important. It's an art form, but you need a broad palette to select from.'

When asked if she has a favourite plant she says no, qualifying this with the fact that the most modest of plants can contribute to the success of a flamboyant neighbour. She also says how the seasons play a part in her favouritism. 'If you come to see me in March and April I'm besotted with hellebores – who isn't then! – and snow-drops, but now in July there is such a plethora that you can't begin to have favourites.' However she did afford herself one special or at least very useful plant, *Helichrysum petiolare* in all its forms. 'It softens everything; without it plantings can look stiff.'

One could say that Beth is used to dealing with large quantities of mature potted plants after her nursery's Chelsea Flower Show exhibits, for which she and her staff won ten consecutive gold medals. She no longer exhibits but admits, 'I loved Chelsea while I was doing it, but it was very hard work physically as I staged the exhibits and humped the pots about. It wasn't only that though, it was also the fact that the preparation took up much of my year. The three months leading up to Chelsea were spent entirely looking after about a thousand potted plants in the busiest time. When I was most needed at home, I was at Chelsea, and all the weeks before when I should have been devoting myself to the nursery were spent doing the Chelsea pots. What finally checked me was when I saw that the garden was going down.

'It was thrilling to put together the exhibit at Chelsea over the years. I would often think that this and that looked so good together, I wished I could be doing the same thing in the garden at home. So I made the decision that I can serve horticulture best by taking care of the garden here during these latter years of my gardening life. And that's what I've been doing for the past four years – "unstitching and knitting" up bits of the original garden.'

MAGNIFICENT MEDLEY

Opposite. *Close by the 'outside dining room', a diversity of plants, individually potted, are grouped, like large living flower arrangements. Great attention is paid to the juxtaposition of colours and textures, with an emphasis on glaucous-leaved succulents. (p.151)*

SUCCULENT STEPS

Above. *From the terrace of the house, flights of steps lead down into the garden. To encourage the less adventurous, a tempting trail of agaves have been placed at intervals, leading the stranger on to explore the delights of Beth Chatto's skilful plant associations, here tinged with silver and purple.*

GHOSTLY PRINTS

Opposite. *On the undersides of the leaves of this agave ghostly marks are clearly visible, made when the foliage was young and* *tightly furled. Now the leaves have spread to capture the morning sun, while beneath trail* Lotus berthelotii. *(p.151)*

A POTTED BORDER

Above. *In a sheltered position a collection of individually potted plants have knitted together to form a summer border. The ornamental grass,* Arundo donax *'Variegata', contributes elegant height to the proceedings, while hydrangeas and petunias compete with one another in the pink stakes. (p.151)*

Rodmarton Manor
The spirit of Arts and Crafts

SIMON AND CHRISTINA BIDDULPH

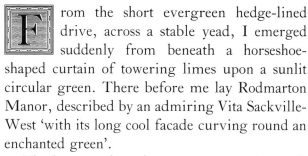

From the short evergreen hedge-lined drive, across a stable yead, I emerged suddenly from beneath a horseshoe-shaped curtain of towering limes upon a sunlit circular green. There before me lay Rodmarton Manor, described by an admiring Vita Sackville-West 'with its long cool facade curving round an enchanted green'.

The house and garden structure are the work of the Cotswold architect Ernest Barnsley. They were built between 1909 and 1926 in the full spirit of the Arts and Crafts Movement, using every local skill available to hand-fashion stone and timber harvested from the estate. In his design of the garden Barnsley constructed a series of architecturally strong 'outdoor rooms' immediately around the house. Further away these became increasingly fragmented to allow for a less restrained form of gardening.

But where are the containers? They are hidden behind this great house, on the sunny south-facing terraces. Some stand in well-ordered isolation while others jostle in lines, like children queuing for their school meals fighting for attention. For other horticultural delicacies of a more

FROM ANIMALS TO ALPINES

Opposite. *Form and formality are combined in the gardens of Rodmarton Manor, as this busy corner shows. A shaft of late afternoon sunlight strikes the angular levels of lichen-dappled stone drinking troughs in Mary Biddulph's 'troughery'.* (p.152)

permanent nature are also taking advantage of this favourable site: large tender shrubs of pittosporum and banksian roses, with autumn-flowering nerines at their feet. This is indeed a garden with an outstanding plant collection.

Rodmarton has been fortunate in having two generations of excellent gardeners: Margaret Biddulph who, with her husband, the Hon. Claud Biddulph, engaged Barnsley; and Mary Biddulph, wife of Major Anthony Biddulph, who inherited the house in 1954. Between them they spent seventy years working to create the gardens we see today. Mary Biddulph died in the summer of 1991 and the estate has now passed to her sons Simon and Jasper. Simon Biddulph, his wife and family have now taken up the Rodmarton reins, and it was to Simon that I talked on a sunny day in high summer.

Simon and Christina are keen to learn and to look after the Manor garden in keeping with the past. I am not sure if he plans to start work in the garden at 5.30 am like his mother, who believed that that was the best time to get the work done! But the old rituals are being carried on: the dividing and replanting of the extensive snowdrop collection and one of the herbaceous borders; the near-constant tending of the vine and fig houses; and the bringing out from the glasshouses of the many half-hardy and tender plants to fill the stone vases and urns on the two broad stone terraces. Backed by the house and topiary-topped angular yew hedges in the best Barnsley 'room' tradition, Mary Biddulph called this her 'parks department'. So colourful and jolly were the urn plantings that they reminded her of local-authority bedding schemes.

These urns of bright pelargoniums and floriferous fuchsias on the first terrace are joined a short distance away by large boxes of agapanthus in blue and white, their long-stemmed flowers swaying in the light breeze. Agapanthus flower well in this hot position, baked by the sun in August and September to prepare them for flowering the following year. 'The boxes were made here from elm trees which had become diseased in the early 1970s. They would have been made up by the estate maintenance department,' points out Simon. And so the fundamental Arts and Crafts ideal of Rodmarton continues.

The second terrace has a quieter theme with more blue and white agapanthus, and I asked Simon what they are planted in: 'The agapanthus containers are plastic forty-five gallon silage chemical containers, cut in half, with rope handles woven through the tops. They make good tubs which are light when empty. When full of agapanthus and compost, Ken, the gardener makes sure they have not been watered for several days before he and his helpers attempt to lift them.' In late autumn these tubs must be transported back to the glasshouses for overwintering.

Away from the terraces, large simple dish-like concrete containers are used on gravel squares, set within paving. Their wide tops make them ideal for massed plantings of abutilons, pelargoniums and other plants which enjoy the warmth and shelter the low pots provide.

Simon's mother had a particular liking for alpine and very small plants. These were given a special home in the 'troughery', a large collection of stone troughs placed at different levels, some on the ground, many perched up on staddle stones of different heights. 'The troughery has evolved over the years but I think it's all post-1950, mainly 1960s,' recollects Simon. 'The troughs were all gathered up from around the farm; originally they would have been used by cattle. The largest, which stands on its own near the winter garden, was my father's pet gardening place. He used to think that was his domain.'

A WELL-FURNISHED 'ROOM'

Opposite. *In this garden 'room' pots, boxes, stone tables and iron-work seats create a lived-in atmosphere. In late summer, the agapanthus do not disappoint. They put on a fine show in their prosaic, but functional, containers.* (p.152)

WITHIN CLIPPED WALLS

Above. *Stone urns are block planted with floriferous fuchsias and pelargoniums to give summer-long colour in the first of two garden 'rooms' – the second is shown opposite – enclosed by immaculately clipped 'walls' of yew.* (p.152)

DRIPPING WITH FLOWERS

Left. *A golden variegated
abutilon glows in the autumn
sunshine. Beneath its foliage,
fuchsias hang low, their
pendulous flowers mimicked by
nearby leycesteria. Here the
simplest of containers recedes into
the background to the benefit of
the planting.* (p.152)

RAISED TO NEW HEIGHTS

Above. *An stone cattle trough is
raised up on staddle stones for
closer examination. Filled with
flowers it provides necessary
colour at the far end of the
'troughery'. In this walled
garden, containers and supports
are as important as their
contents.* (p.153)

HIGH VICTORIAN STYLE
A well-fed garden

SUSAN DICKINSON

shockingly good planting of pillar-box red and acid lime green greets visitors to this late-nineteenth century house in high-Victorian style. Three-foot wide borders run either side of the front door along the house walls, filled with deepest red *Pelargonium* 'Paul Crampel' and *Nicotiana affinis* 'Lime Green' combined with *Canna*, *Ricinus*, *Dahlia* 'Bishop of Llandaff', *Hosta* and *Cordyline*, and backed by the rampant annual growth of *Cobaea scandens* 'Alba'. *Cobaea* make light work of scrambling up the decorative brickwork using their very fine but strong tendrils, almost jeering at the climbing roses that depend upon wires, vine-eyes, string and the gardeners' help to haul them up the walls. The borders are edged with rope-twist tiles which contribute greatly to the Victorian theme. Completing this scene of nineteenth-century ornamentation are the magnificently planted containers arranged around the broad gravel terrace.

Four large terracotta pots, one pair either side of the front door, continue the lime and red theme of the border. Other similar plantings are made in pots well-placed around corners and by windows. When making up the mixed plantings

CHERISHED CHERRIES

Opposite. *Within the unheated Edwardian nectarine house, in early summer, potted dessert cherries share the fan-trained nectarines' protected environment. Warmth from the sun is sufficient to hasten ripening; doors and vents are netted to exclude birds.*

for these pots, nothing is planned on paper; the tall central plant is positioned first and then other plants are added.

The greatest surprise meets you when rounding the end of the house. The mood alters completely, although, again, the terrace pots are planted as part of the overall bedding scheme. Left behind are the powerful colour combinations of the front to be replaced by an equally dramatic display of pink, blue and predominantly white. The plants have been chosen particularly with scent in mind, to surround the terrace where the family like to sit. Here *Tibouchina urvilleana*, *Plumbago capensis* and *Hibiscus* are the central plants surrounded by argyranthemums, pelargoniums, salvias, petunias, myrtle, osteospermums and verbenas, with the different shapes of flowers and leaves used as in a flower arrangement.

The head gardener, Susan Dickinson, has had a distinguished career in horticulture which began with her mother encouraging her to attend one of the last two-year training courses to be held at Waterperry Horticultural School, near Oxford. From there she went to Malahide Castle on the east coast of Ireland, lapped by the waters of the Gulf Stream. Then to the Arboretum at Kalmthout, in Belgium, for a year before returning to England to work at the botanical gardens at Reading University. Opportunities arose for her to work at Hatfield House in Hertfordshire, and then Sissinghurst Castle in Kent before going to garden with Mrs Merton at The Old Rectory, Burghfield.

Mrs Merton and Susan worked closely

together: 'We both enjoy the same style of gardening and she has such a wonderful collection of interesting plants. Mrs Merton's terrace pots have inspired so many people to more adventurous pot planting.

'At Hatfield there were large stone pots in the scented garden, but they were simply planted with scented-leaved pelargoniums, like 'Lady Plymouth' and *Pelargonium tomentosum*. Then at Sissinghurst the plantings in the urns, pots and troughs were again quite simple, using one type of plant in each container; *Acaena*, *Helichrysum*, *Mimulus*, *Pelargonium* 'Lord Bute' and *Impatiens*. Deep purple petunias and grey helichrysums were used together in the top courtyard; and regular watering and feeding was the routine.'

Walking on around the terrace, past richly scented towering *Nicotiana sylvestris*, we came upon large pots of obscenely healthy daturas, dripping with flowers and foliage of deep green. These are fed every day in summer with a high nitrogen liquid fertilizer. They become terribly pot-bound which means on hot windy days they may have to be watered three times. In October they are pruned back by at least half to a structured shape and housed over winter in glasshouses with a minimum temperature of 7°C (45°F). There they are kept watered and fed once a week to keep them just ticking over. In May, they are potted up into bigger containers to give them some new compost. Some young stock is always coming along to replace the oldest plants.

But why, I ask, is there not a sign of the great curse of daturas – red spider mite? 'I think if you keep them growing strongly and in very good health they are nothing like as prone to attack from red spider mites.'

BEDDING AT ITS FINEST

Right. *Large terracotta pots billow with fine plants, red and lime green in flower with purple-leaved cordylines adding contrast. In the adjacent border the theme continues, with the whole magnificent display reaching its climax in late summer.* (p.153)

As you may have gathered, Susan believes strongly in the virtues of liquid feeding which gives her the option to change the formula according to the needs of the plant. She feeds the tree-like *Sparmannia africana* once a day with a high nitrogen fertilizer. This summer, as an experiment, lemon verbenas, heliotropes and petunias were all fed with high nitrogen once a week, and they responded by producing deep green leaves and flowering madly until mid October. Everything else is fed once a week with a high potash liquid fertilizer.

We walk a short distance from the house to reach the stable yard and the walled kitchen garden which is in full production. In the stable yard thirteen tubs are planted identically in white and shades of yellow which go well with the building. Brickwork is used in all the architecture, including the high wall around the kitchen garden. This is why terracotta pots are used almost exclusively, tying in with their surroundings perfectly.

The kitchen garden has been re-designed by Mary Keen and although ornamental, with metalwork arches, decoratively trained fruit, a herb garden and borders for cut flowers and herbaceous perennials, it is a working vegetable garden. Refreshingly basic and honest in layout; Mr McGregor would feel quite at home here!

A triangular area of gravel in front of the peach case, a slim lean-to glasshouse, has become a pot garden. Young orange and lemon trees will, in time, give height to this area which, with the protective south-facing wall behind the box hedging in front, is a lovely place to sit and makes an ideal position for terracotta pots of different shapes and sizes. The composition of a pot or group of pots is based on colour schemes of blue and orange; purple and red; yellow, white and blue; and shades of pink and maroon with white and silver.

In the herb garden four pots are planted with scented-leaved pelargoniums. These are not allowed to flower so the leaf shapes and different shades of green can be enjoyed without distraction. One of the traditions of the garden is to grow a wide range of fruit under glass; and it is in front of one of the glasshouses, in July, that I see cherry trees in large terracotta pots, standing on a gravel parade ground, like ranks of soldiers brought to attention.

These potted dessert cherries produce fine quality fruits early in the year which can be protected from birds. The rigorously pruned cherries, some of them very old, fruit heavily.

Susan explains the cherries' year: 'In February the pots are brought into a cold greenhouse, they come into flower early when there are few pollinating insects about, so they are hand pollinated using a rabbits tail to dust the pollen over the flowers. To keep the trees a manageable size the young shoots are pinched back to four buds. This removes any blackfly which, if present will ruin the fruit. As the cherries begin to swell they are fed with liquid manure, made by soaking a sack of sheep droppings in water. The black cherries fruit first, then the reds and finally the white varieties, to give a fruiting season from the end of May to early July. The trees are then stood outside until the following year.

'The cherries will need re-potting every four years when as much as possible of the old compost is carefully removed from around the roots. Then the trees are re-potted in a homemade mixture of sterilized loam, horticultural sand and leaf-mould, well-broken-up manure and bonemeal made up to the John Innes formula. After a couple of years a "collar" of loam and manure is put around the top of the pot for the feeding roots to get their toes into.'

In years gone by, the cherry pots were transported down to the house, to the dining-room, for guests to pick the fruits from the trees for their dessert – high Victorian style indeed!

FLOWERY FINIALS

Opposite. *To emphasize the head and foot of a series of four flights of terrace steps, pairs of white marble urns – eight pairs in all – surmount short limestone plinths. These lighten the low stone steps adding flowery finials.* (p.153)

SIMULATED SUNSHINE

Above. Argyranthemum
'Jamaica Primrose' bristles with
pale yellow flowers, beneath
which the purest white petunias
unfurl their funnel-like flowers.
This is one of thirteen identically
planted pots which embellish
every aspect of the sheltered
stable yard. (p.154)

PURPLE AND RED

Above. *This heliotrope is called
'Princess Marina', an old
cultivar of excellent colour and
scent. It forms part of larger
composition in the pot garden,
based on a colour scheme of
purple and red, but also
featuring fine combinations of
foliage.* (p.154)

CLASSICAL COMPOSITION

Opposite. *An elegant terrace
where the pendulous trumpets of
datura release their heady scent
for those sitting close by to enjoy.
Morning glory and cobaea
clamber up stonework to unite
house with garden, and adding a
hint of colour to the muted tones
of wickerwork, gravel and
stone.* (p.154)

CONNECTICUT COLOR
From England to New England

GARY KEIM

In New England, in the Litchfield Hills of northwest Connecticut, two well-stocked gardens are tended by keen plantsman Gary Keim. The climate here can be one of extremes with winter temperatures as low as −29C (−20°F) and summers often humid and hot reaching a maximum of 38°C (100°F), however there is a good average rainfall of forty-five inches a year. Many plants will not tolerate this great summer baking and then being frozen in winter, but they can make excellent candidates for container growing.

Gary Keim has been interested in plants and gardens as long as he can remember, cultivating a vegetable garden when very young and planting pots with annuals such as begonias, zonal pelargoniums and impatiens for summer colour. Visits to many public and private gardens and the experience of working at Longwood Gardens, Pennsylvannia, opened his eyes to the immense possibilities that container gardening could offer. This was reinforced by nine months of studying in England. As Gary told me, 'It provided immeasurable inspiration both for the vast array of plants which can be used in containers, and for

the heights of sophistication which can be achieved.' Upon his return to the United States he began working in the two New England gardens where he is fortunate in having a free hand to experiment with containers, which play a significant role in both gardens.

Gary's style of gardening is similar to my own: namely he prefers a strong almost formal garden structure of well-defined lines. The planting used within this is rich and luxuriant and serves to soften the edges, giving a pleasant contrast.

'I like many types of plants and enjoy seeing them "cheek by jowl". I combine the many qualities of plants, such as flower and leaf colour, overall shape and texture, and flowering period, to pull the whole garden together.' Gary goes on to say of colour: 'My colour combinations run the gamut, ranging from quiet associations of soft tints to screaming mixes of hot colours. Generally I tend to lean towards brighter colours. I find them exciting and powerful, due partially I think to the fact that other gardeners avoid them.'

The majority of his containers are of terracotta. 'It ages so nicely and provides such a good foil for most plants.' He also uses cast-iron planters and baskets, as well as those of concrete. Gary makes some observations on the planting of containers: 'I plant my pots so as they look sparse at the onset of the season. With adequate watering and feeding they are quick to fill in and knit together, creating a desirable effect after a short time which will improve and mature as the season progresses. I also stagger my plantings to give a continuity of pots peaking throughout the season.

PANSY PEBBLE POT

Opposite. *The aptly named pansies, 'Jolly Joker' and 'Spanish Sun', sit brightly in this unusual container, their small flowers raised to survey the meadow-like surroundings. Such a delightful combination is well suited to a wildlife garden.* (p.154)

Weekly "preening" of the plantings is essential to remove dead and yellowing leaves and flowers.'

It is interesting to see how our shrinking world has even touched the planting of containers; for Gary lists among his favourites many container plants familiar in Europe: '*Verbena canadensis* cultivars, *Verbena* 'Sissinghurst' and 'Silver Anne', scented-leaved pelargoniums, the small-leaved *Helichrysum* now called *Plectostachys serphyllifolia*, *Oxypetalum caeruleum* (perhaps better known as *Tweedia caerulea*), the Pearl series of *Petunia*, New Zealand flax or *Phormium*, and the chocolate plant, *Cosmos atrosanguineus*. At present I'm really taken by the genus *Salvia*, I grow *Salvia discolor* and *Salvia chiapensis*, both excellent container contributors, and my experiments continue with any other species which comes my way. *Diascia* too, are favourites and quite new to American horticulture. *Diascia* 'Ruby Field', *Diascia fetcaniensis* and *Diascia* 'Pink Queen' have proved invaluable. They have quickly become staples in my repertoire. This year two plants new to me which I like a lot are *Scaevola aemula* 'Blue Wonder', a lush tender plant from Australia which has masses of mid-blue spikes of flowers rather like a large lobelia, and *Petunia integrifolia* var. *integrifolia* whose flowers are borne freely in shades of purple. It is one of the parents of our modern-day petunias. *Scaevola* and *Petunia* are both wonderful weavers, threading nicely through silvers and greys.'

Gary groups the pots together to form a border or small garden of their own, giving splashes of colour just where they are needed. He plays with colour to maximize impact of a group, either by tying in with plants growing in the garden proper or by taking advantage of the detached nature of a container allowing the contents to 'revolt' (his word) against their local surroundings.

A recent experiment with water-absorbing polymers has given very pleasing results. These hold water in the compost, providing an available 'reservoir' to the plant over a long period of time. This is something Gary will be using a lot more of in the future in his exciting schemes for container gardening.

BATHED IN COLOUR

Opposite. *Duel colour combinations run against each other with cheerful consequences. In the border white tobacco plants and yellow lilies scent the evening air, while round the bird bath sit pots of mixed petunias and verbenas. (p.155)*

SUPPORTING ROLE

Above. *Standing against an iron railing a terracotta pot is buried beneath the delicate flowers of* Convolvulus sabatius *and a purple verbena. Although in no way a major planting, such attractive small features add charm to a garden. (p.154)*

A Collector's Contribution

Opposite. *Carefully arranged pots on paving, resemble an eighteenth-century collector's nature table. Instead of exotic seeds and fruit, living plants of associated colouring are laid out to be studied. The garden chairs add to the feeling that these plants should be taken seriously. (p.155)*

A Spiky Statement

Above. *A terracotta pots sits on a stone pier within a flower garden full of the vivid colours favoured by Gary Keim. Equally vivid are the flowers of this species petunia, whose dainty growths twist and turn below the slender spikes of a cordyline. Cordylines are superb plants for pots, adding airy height and structure to any composition. (p.155)*

SOUTHVIEW
A taste of winter

RUPERT GOLBY

My own garden in Oxfordshire is mercifully small and therefore, for me, rather a treat as a morning's work here can provide some pleasing overall progress. In some of the larger gardens in which I work, a week of toil can very easily be lost to all but the keenest of eyes. Despite my lack of rolling acres, I enjoy growing a wide range of plants. These are packed into borders against old stone walls, and beneath fruit trees that have seen better days. To allow myself extra room for plants which often deserve close scrutiny, I have many containers of different sizes, shapes and materials.

A wide stone ledge immediately opposite the kitchen windows provides an ideal west-facing display area, where containers sporting their finest are massed together for colour, shape or form. They are rearranged and replenished with fresher container-grown plants as the seasons advance. The stone ledge is well stocked right through the year, and looks attractive even in mid-winter, when potted box shapes, young *Hamamelis × intermedia* 'Arnold Promise' and winter-flowering *Viburnum × bodnantense* 'Dawn' put on a good show.

GALLANT GALANTHUS

Opposite. *In the dark days of February, a snow-encrusted trough of snowdrops lifts the heart. Hidden beneath the snow are the silvery rosettes of* Glaucium flavum. *Leafy rosettes of* Silybum marianum *would make equally suitable companions. (p.156)*

To plant containers for a winter show, two important considerations must be taken into account. Firstly, the severity of the winter weather and, secondly, the fact that plants do not grow through the winter months. Only the hardiest of plants and containers of proven frost resistance should be used. One must bear in mind that a compost and root-filled container is exposed to severe weather not just in a single plane, as with the surface of a border, but in three dimensions. Hence a container will freeze through when a border will only have a crust of frozen soil. A fragile pot, or a plant of borderline hardiness will, therefore, not survive many spells of temperatures which, day and night, do not rise above freezing. A container planting for winter must be hardier than any other planting in the garden as it must stand proud, with top growth and root system taking the full force of winter.

It may seem I am stating the obvious when I say plants do not grow in winter. However, unlike a spring-planted summer pot where plants grow to fill and overflow by late summer, a winter pot must be planted in its final form in the autumn, when plant growth has all but ceased. It must be of preformed, prefabricated design; flowering plants such as wallflowers, forget-me-nots or winter pansies cannot be depended upon to develop further their extent or form. They will merely give a green salad effect across the top of the container, and height and spread will only be successfully achieved by using hardy evergreen or deciduous shrubs with some winter virtue. I use box, *Buxus sempervirens*, in many of my winter plantings, it has a depth of green unusual in winter. Box has a size of leaf small enough to look appropriate in scale in the smallest of containers, it can be allowed to grow in its natural loose form or clipped as a shape. Collections of simple box balls grown together can look particularly amusing. Small-leaved ivies, many of the cultivars of *Hedera helix*, will furnish the surface and sides of containers, and, in partnership with box, will make a pleasing combination.

Portuguese laurel (*Prunus lusitanica*), golden and silver variegated holly (*Ilex* cultivars), clipped yew and privet shapes, elaeagnus, osmanthus, viburnum and many other tough evergreen shrubs are suitable for winter pots. Smaller evergreens might include *Helleborus foetidus* and *H. argutifolius*, periwinkle (*Vinca minor* and *V. major*), small-leaved hebes and *Euonymus* cultivars. Some deciduous shrubs can be used: the dogwoods, in particular, *Cornus stolonifera* 'Flaviramea' which has lime green stems. Some willows also have bright stem colour, *Salix alba* 'Hutchinson's Yellow' for instance; and others, like *S. aegyptiaca*, are resplendent with silvery 'pussy willow' flowers in February and March. The corkscrew hazel, *Corylus avellana* 'Contorta', provides amusement with its wriggling twisting stems and catkins in February.

With the shapes of interest in place it is then time to embellish with overlays of colour in the form of early spring bulbs planted in layers: the latest-flowering, largest bulbs lowest in the planter, and the smallest, earliest bulbs near the surface. Above these bulbs, at the surface, traditional winter bedding may be added amongst the shapes. Forget-me-nots (*Myosotis*), daisies (*Bellis perennis*), wallflowers (*Cheiranthus*) for example, all give extra spring colour and finish the planting by covering any bare compost; the bulbs beneath will force their way through.

Sometimes I use the over-wintering stage of a biennial plant which will be usually in the form of a flat ground-hugging rosette and can look very attractive. The most decorative would be some of the thistle-like plants: *Galactites tomentosa*, with its silver-veined, rich green leaves and *Silybum marianum*, mottled and veined like Italian marble, – both look wonderful with snowdrops. Overwintering *Verbascum olympicum*, a mullein covered in silver hairs, is also very attractive, as are the yellow-splashed leaves of the variegated land-cress, *Barbarea vulgaris* 'Variegata'. *Lamium maculatum* 'Beacon Silver' and *Valeriana phu* 'Aurea' can also be used in this way.

I find it necessary to water the containers, even if they are planted up on a cold wet day in October, to establish the individual root-balls within the new compost. Thereafter they should be checked weekly and watered if dry. It is surprising how evergreen plants will prevent rain reaching the compost and if containers are placed against the wall of a house, very little rain will ever reach them. Because the plants are not growing until the spring, the feeding of winter pots is unnecessary.

In the most acute winter weather I carry pots of manageable size and weight into an unheated shed or garage. Those containers too big to move I put straw bales around or wrap them up, plants and all, in hessian, after firstly pushing long canes around the edge of the pot. Another alternative is to push in branches of conifer around the plants as an insulation. These precautions rarely need to be left in place for more than a week at a time, and perhaps used only twice in one winter, when temperatures below freezing persist through the day to the following night.

A winter planting may not have the spectacular ebullience of a summer pot, but when all else in the garden lies bleak and bare, a wooden tub of frost-encrusted evergreens sparkling in early morning sunshine has a very special charm – especially with the promise of snowdrops, and spring to come.

SAGE GREEN ICICLES

Opposite. The colours of the catkins and the rich green foliage of Garrya elliptica *'James Roof' are the inspiration behind the choice of plants that grow in the small copper container: hellebores, ivies, and* Osmaronia cerasiformis. *(p.156)*

WARM TONES IN WINTER

Left. Viburnum×bodnantense
'Dawn' plays host to a richly
planted, weathered urn. Bead-
like buds of skimmia glow
against the red-tipped foliage of
photinia. (p.156)

VERDANT COPPER

Above. *A large copper bulges
with greenery in the depth of
winter.* Salix 'Kilmarnock'
*showers silver 'pussy' flowers
onto the evergreens below and
Arum italicum, with strongly
veined leaves, surrounds the pot.*
(p.156)

THE APPROACH OF SPRING

Right. *As the last winter snow thaws, signs of spring are revealed with the expanding inflorescences of hellebores. Crocuses have pushed their way through cold soil but need the sun to open wide their flowers. (p.157)*

BOXED BALLS

Above. *A fine Tuscan terracotta box is simply planted with clipped box balls and ivy. Unfortunately, terracotta boxes and troughs are vulnerable in frosty weather when frozen compost expands, splitting the corners apart. (p.157)*

FOR CHRISTMAS

Opposite. *At the very end of the year a shallow oval basket pot, planted in November, gives a Christmas treat to last into the New Year. The blooms of Narcissus 'Paper White' will fill a room with their heavenly perfume, but the plant does have one major drawback. Due to its rapid growth it tends to flop over, especially when brought into a warm room. Here twigs of contorted willow are used to give decorative support. (p.157)*

ORIENTAL MAGIC

Above. *Pale green and white has a freshness few colour combinations can match and looks particularly good against terracotta. The star of this display is* Helleborus orientalis, *perfect and unblemished. If hellebores are to be grown successfully in containers they will need a heavy loamy compost with added grit for good drainage. During summer, shade must be provided; they are best stood beneath a tree or large shrub, or against a north-facing wall. (p.157)*

Part Two

THE PLANTING DETAILS

My very first recollections of container planting in gardens are of agapanthus and agaves in plain Victorian flowerpots, stood out for the summer in my grandparents' garden. In the cold greenhouse, rows of unusual-coloured Primula auricula *in 'long-tom' pots were displayed on old-fashioned staging. In my parents' garden I would fill large disused china 'Belfast' sinks with bulbs to produce a riot of colour in spring.*

It was not until later that the intricacies of multiple plantings became part of my own repertoire. These I first saw planted in the South Cottage garden at Sissinghurst Castle, Kent, where a large hot-water copper was filled with glowing red tulips for spring and vibrant Mimulus glutinosus *for summer.*

On the pages that follow, the more complicated planting combinations illustrated in Part One are set out in detail and may be used in conjunction with the List of Suppliers, *on page 158, to recreate any of the displays illustrated. The container considerations, overleaf, have been drawn up to provide the gardener with a concise checklist of useful information — from choosing a container to the aftercare of a mature display.*

Opposite. *A strong combination of plants, put together by Phillip Watson, where foliage triumphs over flower. The golden striations of the bamboos create their own sunlight, while dark coleus makes its own dense shadows. (p.147)*

When container gardening there are many details worthy of consideration before and after the purchase of a new pot, and in planting and caring for the display. Space here is limited and so I have been able to offer only brief notes but I hope they will answer most basic questions.

CONTAINER SELECTION

Before choosing a new container, think carefully about the following points. The overall size of the container should be in scale with the intended surroundings. The colour and material should link with the adjacent stonework, brickwork or woodwork. Is the container to stand alone or in a group? A group of similar containers give unity rather than many varied styles. Decide on whether an ornate or simple style is best suited to the intended location; containers should be associated with the house or the garden architecture. For plants with large root systems, choose flared rimmed pots to allow root-bound plants to be extracted easily.

SOAKING AND AGEING TERRACOTTA
AND STONEWARE

In summer new terracotta and stoneware containers must be soaked to absorb water before planting and so avoid the pots 'robbing' the compost of water.

The strong tones of red terracotta may be 'calmed' if an application of dry garden lime is sprinkled onto a damp pot. Repeated wetting of the pot with a hand mister and the colour will quickly pale. Lichen can be encouraged to form on terracotta and stoneware with an application of dilute manure.

REDUCING WATER-LOSS

To reduce evaporation through the stone and terracotta, a clear sealer may be applied to the inner wall of the container, sealing the pores. This also reduces frost damage as it prevents water, which may freeze, from entering the container material. A polythene bag can be used to line a container reducing water-loss – particularly useful in a wall pot where evaporation can be excessive, but remember to puncture some holes in the bottom to allow water to drain.

COMPOST

All my contributors have reduced the amount of peat they use in their composts, and at Kew no peat is used at all. Coir or cocofibre can be added to loam-based general potting composts in place of peat. The best known loam-based compost is that made to the John Innes formula. More recently general-purpose composts have come onto the market, made possible by the advent of reliable longlife, slow-release fertilizers. The loam-based forms seem to be taking over from John Innes, thereby removing the necessity to hold composts of three different strengths.

DRAINAGE

If ample drainage is not provided, the compost can become waterlogged, depriving roots of air, causing death and rotting. Covering the drainage hole is not sufficient. Use at least two layers (four to five inches in a large container) of a flat material, such as broken pots, tiles or slates, to allow through water, but not compost. Fine chippings or gravel will quickly become blocked with compost. In an exposed site extra stability may be given to a pot by using large stones and half-bricks as drainage material to give added weight. On roof gardens, where weight can be a disadvantage, use pieces of broken polystyrene to a depth of six to eight inches in a large pot.

If saucers are to be used beneath containers, care must be taken not to over-water, as pots sitting in water mean root-death to plants.

PLANTING

Part-fill the pot with compost to a depth determined by the rootball of the largest plant, so that when the rootballs are placed on the compost surface their tops are just below the rim of the container. When the plants are positioned satisfactorily, fill in around the rootballs with more compost. If annual bedding plants are used, large pots need not be emptied entirely each year. Remove the root-filled top eight-inches or so and replace with fresh compost. Every four years empty the pot completely and refill with new compost.

WATERING AND FEEDING

Once planted and in position, water thoroughly until excess water flows from the bottom of the container. Use a rose on a hose or watering-can so the compost is settled gently. Containers should be checked daily; in hot weather small pots will need daily watering, larger pots three times a week. Once a week add a liquid fertilizer to the can or hose-diluter, watering over the plants to feed foliage as well as roots. Slow-release fertilizer granules or plugs may be added to the surface of the compost to release nutrients each time water occurs.

AFTERCARE AND WINTERCARE

It is essential to deadhead flowering plants, not only to improve the appearance of the planting, but in order to encourage continuous flowering until autumn.

For details of wintercare please see pages 127–128.

THE OLD RECTORY
Annie Huntington

Due to the large number of containers to be filled in spring and autumn, the Huntington's find it necessary to use bought potting compost sparingly. The large containers are partially filled with two-year-old, well-rotted garden compost, and then topped up with a 50:50 mixture of loam-based compost and multi-purpose cocofibre compost to a depth of at least one foot.

A handful of bonemeal is incorporated into the garden compost towards the bottom of the pot to give sustenance to those plants with deep roots. A liquid fertilizer is applied to each container once a week throughout the summer.

Page 1	Photographed 28 April

CONTAINER
Type oak half-barrel
Size height 15 inches, width 28 inches
Age 5 years

PLANTING
Permanently planted evergreen shrubs and bulbs, primarily for winter and spring display.
Position open courtyard, partially shaded by trees

Key to plants
1. 1 *Buxus sempervirens* (clipped as a ball)
2. 15 *Tulipa* 'Spring Green'
3. 3 *Hebe rakaiensis*
4. 1 *Hedera helix* 'Nymans'
5. pink tulips from a previous year's display

Page 16	Photographed 28 April

CONTAINER
Type double rimmed terracotta pot
Size height 10 inches, width 19 inches
Age 5 years

PLANTING
An autumn-planted pot for winter/spring effect, using herbaceous plants, sub-shrubs and bulbs.
Position west-facing courtyard

Key to plants
1. 20 *Tulipa* 'Bleu Aimable'
2. 1 *Ruta graveolens* 'Jackman's Blue'
3. 8 *Heuchera micrantha* 'Palace Purple'

Page 19	Photographed 28 April

GROUP PLANTING
A collection of pots planted with herbaceous perennials, biennials and bulbs planted in autumn for spring display.
Position west-facing

CONTAINER A
Type scalloped terracotta bowl
Size height 9 inches, width 17 inches
Age 5 years

Key to plants
1. 1 *Valeriana phu* 'Aurea'
2. 3 *Tanacetum parthenium* 'Aureum'
3. 3 *Primula* 'Alan Robb'

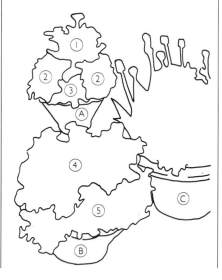

CONTAINER B
Type scalloped terracotta bowl
Size height 9 inches, width 17 inches
Age 5 years

Key to plants
4. 5 *Silybum marianum*
5. 5 *Phlox stolonifera* 'Ariane'

CONTAINER C
See description for page 16

Page 21 (left)	Photographed 10 July

GROUP PLANTING
A mixed display of bulbs and tender plants for summer enjoyment.
Position west-facing courtyard

CONTAINER A
Type plain, wide-rimmed terracotta pot
Size height 13 inches, width 19 inches
Age 7 years

Plants 10 *Lilium* 'Capitol' (planted in autumn)

CONTAINER B
Type double rimmed pot
Size height 10 inches, width 19 inches
Age 5 years

Plants 5 *Pelargonium* 'Tip Top Duet' (planted in spring)

CONTAINER C
Type terracotta olive pot
Size 10 inches, width 12 inches
Age 5 years

Plants 3 *Pelargonium* 'Brown's Butterfly' (planted in spring)

CONTAINER D
Also see photograph on page 20
Type double-rimmed terracotta pot
Size height 10 inches, width 19 inches
Age 5 years

Key to plants
1. 3 *Rhodochiton atrosanguineus*
2. 3 *Pelargonium* 'Tip Top Duet'

CONTAINER

Type plain wide-rimmed terracotta pot
Size height 13 inches, width 19 inches
Age 7 years

PLANTING

A spring-planted summer pot of tender plants.
Position within a north-facing border

Key to plants
1. 3 *Pelargonium* 'Bird Dancer'
2. 1 *Argyranthemum foeniculaceum*
3. *Lamium maculatum* 'White Nancy' (in border)

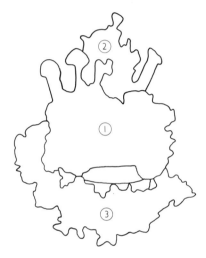

CONTAINER

Type terracotta pastry terrace pot
Size height 22 inches, width 30 inches
Age 2 years

PLANTING

An autumn-planted spring pot containing bulbs and an evergreen shrub.
Position west-facing courtyard

Key to plants
1. 1 *Buxus sempervirens* 'Elegantissima'
2. 20 *Narcissus* 'Rippling Waters'
3. 20 *Tulipa* 'Angelique'
4. *Dicentra spectabilis* (in border)

BARNSLEY HOUSE
Rosemary Verey

As many thousands of plants are propagated and potted up for sale at Barnsley House each year, a good but low-cost compost is important. So the hen-run was turned to for help with the job. All the organic garden and kitchen waste which the hens will eat or which will break down into compost is spread over the floor of the run (taking care not to include any poisonous material, such as hellebore seeds).

Once a year the run, which will have reached two foot high in poultry droppings and organic material, is cleared and the material stacked.

After a year the stack is wheel-barrowed into a barn to dry. When the stack has dried out sufficiently the material is then sieved and mixed in equal parts with the peaty compost of 'spent' growing-bags. Perlite is added at the rate of one part by volume to every eight parts compost, together with a little organic fertilizer. The mixture is then turned twice to blend thoroughly, and this is the compost used in all the Barnsley House containers.

Throughout the summer a liquid feed is applied, once a fortnight, to all the occupants of the Barnsley House tubs and pots.

GROUP PLANTING

A group of pots for summer display, planted in spring with a selection of tender perennials and fuchsias.
Position east-facing terrace, backed by the house

CONTAINER A

Type oak half-barrel
Size height 15 inches, width 28 inches
Age 3 years

Key to plants
1. 1 *Pelargonium* 'Best Mauve' (syn. *P.* 'La France')
2. 3 *Pelargonium graveolens*
3. 5 *Petunia* white F$_1$ hybrid
4. 5 *Viola* 'Belmont Blue'
5. 4 *Helichrysum petiolare*
6. *Sedum* 'Bertram Anderson'

OTHER CONTAINERS

Type terracotta flower pots
Sizes height 10–13 inches, width 11–12 inches
Age nineteenth century

Key to plants
7. *Pelargonium* 'Lady Plymouth'
8. *Fuchsia* 'Checkerboard' (trained as a standard)
9. *Pelargonium* 'Hederinum'
10. *Diascia stachyoides*
11. *Salvia rutilans*
12. *Pelargonium* × *fragrans*
13. *Euonymus fortunei radicans* (in border)

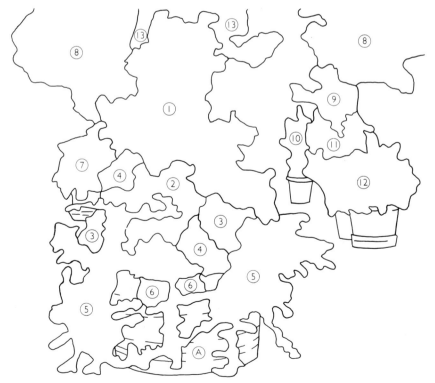

Page 27   *Photographed 18 June*

GROUP PLANTING
Each pan is planted with a pattern of herbs for permanent or semi-permanent display.
Position   sunny south-facing terrace

CONTAINER A
Type   terracotta basketwork pan
Size   height 6 inches, width 23 inches
Age   2 years

Key to plants
1. 1 *Buxus sempervirens* (clipped to a ball)
2. 8 *Thymus × citriodorus* 'Golden Lemon'
3. 4 *Thymus × citriodorus* 'Silver Queen'
4. 14 *Teucrium × lucidrys* (syn. *T. chamaedrys*)
5. 12 *Thymus × citriodorus* 'Aureus'

CONTAINER B
Type   plain terracotta pan
Size   height 4 inches, width 13 inches
Age   nineteenth century

Key to plants
6. 3 *Allium schoenoprasum* (chives)
7. 7 *Thymus* 'Doone Valley'

CONTAINER C
Type   plain English terracotta pan
Size   height 3 inches, width 11 inches
Age   nineteenth century

Key to plants
8. 1 *Buxus sempervirens* (clipped to a ball shape)
9. 3 *Thymus × citriodorus* 'Silver Queen'
10. 7 *Thymus × citriodorus* 'Golden Lemon'

Page 28   *Photographed 4 March*

CONTAINER
Type   oak half-barrel
Size   height 15 inches, width 28 inches
Age   3 years

PLANTING
A winter and spring display of evergreens, herbaceous perennials and bulbs, planted in spring.
Position   east-facing terrace, near the house

Key to plants
1. 1 *Ilex × altaclerensis* 'Golden King'
2. 25 *Narcissus papyraceus*
3. 25 *Tulipa* 'Dillenburg'
4. 100 *Crocus* (mixed)
5. 3 *Vinca minor* 'Gertrude Jekyll'

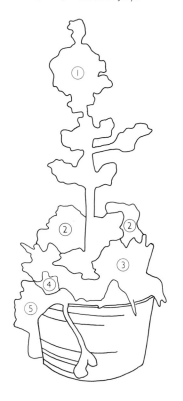

Page 29   *Photographed 18 June*

GROUP PLANTING
A summer pot containing foliage plants planted in spring and a single clipped evergreen shrub.
Position   the foot of an east-facing wall

CONTAINER A
Type   patterned terracotta pot
Size   height 12 inches, width 15 inches
Age   4 years

Key to plants
1. 3 *Milium effusum aureum*
2. 3 *Foeniculum vulgare purpureum*
3. 4 *Viola labradorica*
4. 2 *Lonicera japonica* 'Aureoreticulata'

CONTAINER B
Type   Italian terracotta box
Size   height, width and depth 12 inches
Age   18 years

Plant   *Buxus sempervirens* (trained as a spiral)

Page 30   *Photographed 19 July*

GROUP PLANTING
Permanent planting of evergreen, semi-evergreen and tender shrubs.
Position   northwest-facing corner of the house

CONTAINER A
Type   English terracotta flowerpot
Size   height 13 inches, width 13 inches
Age   nineteenth century

Plant   *Datura suaveolens* (syn. *Brugmansia suaveolens*)

CONTAINER B
Type   wooden Versailles box
Size   height 17 inches, width and depth 19 inches
Age   5 years

Key to plants
1. 1 *Euonymus fortunei* 'Emerald 'n' Gold' (standard)
2. 4 *Lonicera pileata*

CONTAINER
Type oak half-barrel
Size height 15 inches, width 28 inches
Age 3 years

PLANTING
An autumn-planted tub for winter and spring display, with evergreens, herbaceous perennials and bulbs.
Position east-facing terrace

Key to plants
1. 1 *Ilex aquifolium* 'Silver Queen'
2. 25 *Narcissus* 'Soleil d'Or'
3. 25 *Tulipa* 'China Pink'
4. 5 *Vinca minor* 'Aureovariegata'
5. 100 *Crocus* (mixed)

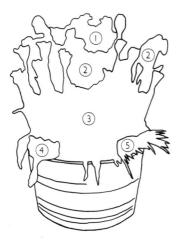

A FULHAM TOWN HOUSE
Helen Preston

In her small London garden there is no room for heaps of rotting turf, or piles of leafmould and grit, so Helen Preston buys a loam-based compost of John Innes No. 3 composition.

Through the summer she feeds her container plants weekly with a liquid feed made from a powdered concentrate. Her pots of lilies are fed long after the flowers have faded, to ensure plump bulbs for the following year.

CONTAINER
Type cylindrical terracotta pot decorated with vines
Size height 10 inches, width 16 inches
Age new

PLANTING
A summer planting of pink, purple and cream foliage and flowers to compliment the tones of the pot.
Position warm, sunny walled garden

Key to plants
1. 1 *Berberis thunbergii* 'Harlequin'
2. 3 *Erigeron karvinskianus*
3. 4 *Ajuga reptans* 'Burgundy Glow'
4. 3 *Allium christophii*

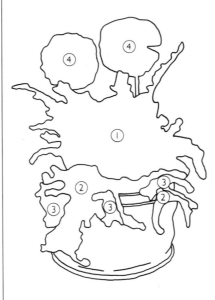

CONTAINER
Type cylindrical lead planter with fielded borders
Size height 11 inches, width 13 inches
Age nineteenth century

PLANTING
To complement the flat lead finish, a range of blue-flowered perennials are used together in this summer-planted pot.
Position warm and sheltered with partial shade from nearby tree

Key to plants
1. 1 *Heliotropium* 'Chatsworth'
2. 3 *Campanula isophylla*
3. 2 *Convolvulus sabatius*

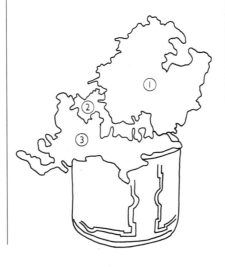

CONTAINER
Type terracotta scroll jardinière
Size height 15 inches, width 14 inches
Age new

PLANTING
A summer planting of tender, peach-toned flowers and foliage.
Position against an east-facing wall

Key to plants
1. 2 *Argyranthemum* 'Peachy Cheeks'
2. 2 *Verbena* 'Peaches and Cream'
3. 2 *Corydalis cheilanthifolia*

CHATSWORTH
Her Grace the Duchess of Devonshire

A compost based on the John Innes No. 2 formula and made at Chatsworth is used to fill all the containers. In the autumn, turf is 'floated off' – a turf float is used to remove an inch-and-a-half-thick layer of grass, topsoil and roots – and stacked for twelve months. It is then thoroughly refined by putting it through a shredder. The resulting loam is mixed and turned to incorporate added peat and horticultural sand, with addition of a base fertilizer. The result is a light, moisture-retentive compost which has proved well-suited to long-term plantings such as citrus and bay trees.

Six to eight weeks after potting or repotting in the spring, containers are top-dressed with bonemeal and dried blood.

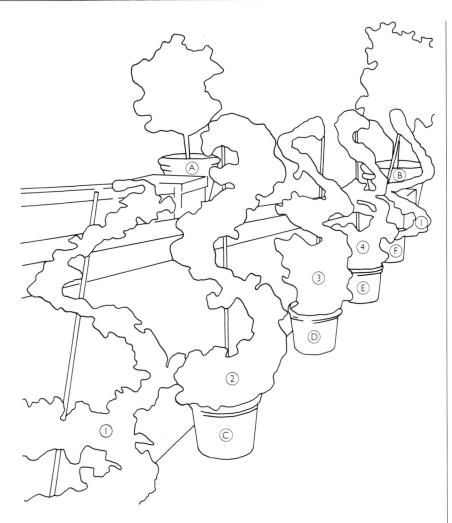

Page 47	Photographed 8 August

CONTAINER
Type cast-iron cauldron
Size height 24 inches, width 27 inches
Age probably pre-1900

PLANTING
Seasonal planting of vegetables.
Position west-facing slope of vegetable garden

Key to plants
1. 1 cabbage
2. 10 French beans
3. 2 gourds (in border)

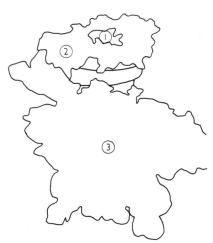

Page 40	Photographed 18 August

GROUP PLANTING
A display of standard lemon trees and hardy ivies spirally trained on a wire and cane support.
Summer position for citrus fairly sheltered, on the east side of the house
Winter position for citrus under glass
Position for *Hedera* in the open all the year round

CONTAINERS A, B
Type Italian terracotta orange pots
Size height 24 inches, width 28 inches
Age 2 years

Plants *Citrus limon* (one per pot)

CONTAINERS C, D, E, F
Type standard terracotta flowerpots
Size height 10 inches, width 13 inches
Age 5 years

Key to plants
1. 1 *Hedera helix* 'Glacier'
2. 1 *Hedera helix* 'Boscoop'
3. 1 *Hedera helix* 'Pittsburg'
4. 1 *Hedera helix* 'Parsley Crested'

Page 44	Photographed 18 August

CONTAINERS
Type wooden Chatsworth boxes
Size 24 inches square
Age 7 years

PLANTING
Standard bay trees for permanent display.
Summer position south-facing at front of the house
Winter position under glass

Plants *Laurus nobilis* (clipped)

Page 46	Photographed 18 August

CONTAINER
Type texture-painted, cast-iron window box
Size height 2 foot, depth 1½ foot, length 7 foot
Age early nineteenth century

PLANTING
A summer display of flowering pelargoniums, planted in spring.
Position sun-baked, south-facing wall of house

A WILTSHIRE MANOR HOUSE
Melanie Chambers
The large containers of lead, stone and copper displayed around the garden are filled with a mixture of loam-based compost (John Innes No. 2), coir peat-substitute and perlite. Coir provides an excellent medium for the fibrous roots of

many annual plants, while perlite keeps the compost open and allows water to drain through freely.

The hungry feeders, like daturas and argyranthemums, are fed twice a week with a liquid tomato fertilizer. Other plants are fed once a week with a balanced liquid fertilizer.

Page 48 *Photographed 24 July*

CONTAINER
Type lead cistern
Size height 28 inches, width 38 inches, depth 21 inches
Age 1755

PLANTING
A collection of tender perennials with a yellow and orange theme, planted in spring for summer display.
Position sheltered courtyard, against a north-facing wall

Key to plants
1. 3 *Argyranthemum* 'Jamaica Primrose'
2. 1 *Eccremocarpus scaber*
3. 1 *Argyranthemum* 'Prado'
4. 2 *Bidens ferulifolia*
5. 3 *Mimulus aurantiacus puniceus*
6. 3 *Mimulus aurantiacus*

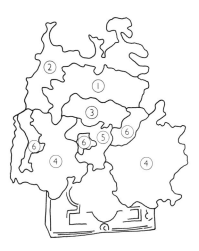

Page 50 *Photographed 25 June*

CONTAINER
Type hot-water copper, made of copper
Size height 23 inches, width 40 inches
Age Victorian

PLANTING
Flowering and foliage plants planted in spring for summer display.
Position centre of a small protected courtyard, with good light

Key to plants
1. 10 *Viola* 'Baby Lucia'
2. 6 *Pelargonium* 'Atomic Snowflake'

3. 4 *Pelargonium* 'Blandfordianum'
4. 4 *Pelargonium* 'Arctic Star'
5. 4 *Glechoma hederacea* 'Variegata'
6. 8 *Hedera helix* 'Hazel'

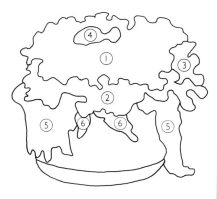

Page 51 *Photographed 25 June*

CONTAINER
Type D-shaped stone trough
Size height 19 inches, width 34 inches
Age pre-1850

PLANTING
A display of tender perennial and climbers planted in spring.
Position east-facing, in a sheltered courtyard

Key to plants
1. 3 *Lathyrus* 'Beaujolais'
2. 2 *Cosmos atrosanguineus*
3. 3 *Pelargonium* 'Lord Bute'
4. 3 *Verbena* 'Sissinghurst'
5. 1 *Salvia discolor*
6. 2 *Plectostachys serpyllifolia*

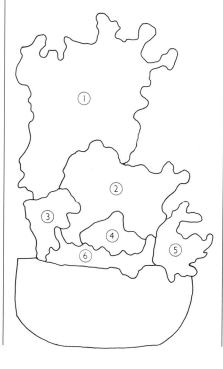

ELTON HALL
Mr and Mrs William Proby

The containers at Elton have been filled traditionally with a peat-based potting compost. However, I have a feeling that in future, with a new head gardener at the helm, of Scottish blood and horticultural training, the peat will stay on the hills and a similar medium, such as cocofibre compost, will take its place in the pots. The reconstituted-stone containers require frequent watering, as the clipped box balls are thirsty and the compost dries out quickly.

A blood, fish and bone fertilizer is stirred into the surface of the compost of each pot in March, and again in May.

Pages 54–57 *Photographed 1 August*

CONTAINER
Type reconstituted-stone vase with draped decoration
Size height 16 inches, width 20 inches
Age 2 years

PLANTING
A permanent planting of a single evergreen.
Position west-facing

Plants *Buxus sempervirens* 'Suffruticosa' (one per pot and clipped to shape)

Page 60 *Photographed 1 August*

CONTAINER
Type Italian terracotta pot decorated with swags
Size height 17 inches, width 19 inches
Age new

PLANTING
A young climber permanently planted to grow over a frame of willow.
Position sheltered

Plants 1 *Convolvulus elegantissimus* and *Origanum laevigatum* (in border)

Page 61 *Photographed 1 August*

CONTAINER
Type built-in stucco planter
Size height 21 inches, width 36 inches, depth 26 inches
Age c. 1860

PLANTING
A permanently planted shrub enlivened by summer bedding.
Position northwest facing with little sun

Key to plants
1. 1 *Cornus alba* 'Elegantissima'
2. 2 *Pelargonium* cv.
3. 2 *Senecio bicolor cineraria*

4. 4 *Lobelia* cv.
5. 4 *Petunia* (mixed)

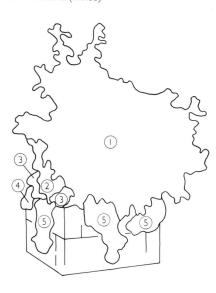

WASHINGTON GARDENS
Phillip Watson

The containers planted by Phillip Watson are filled with his own soil-less mixture. This contains a little Canadian moss peat, but substituting ground pine bark where possible, and dehydrated manure. These ingredients are mixed with vermiculite, perlite and builders' sand to create an open free-draining medium with a high humus content to retain some moisture. Phillip has tried, but does not like, water-absorbing polymers mixed with the compost; he believes that in wet weather these polymers keep the compost too wet for too long. Instead he prefers to apply an organic mulch over the top of the compost to conserve moisture.

The pots are fed once a week with a diluted liquid fertilizer concentrate.

Page 62	Photographed 8 July

CONTAINER
Type terracotta bowl
Size height 7 inches, width 16 inches
Age 4 years

PLANTING
A summer display of mixed perennials, planted in spring.
Position full sun

Key to plants
1. 2 *Saliva ferruginea* 'Porcelain'
2. 1 *Salvia farinacea* 'Victoria'
3. 2 *Verbena tenuisecta* 'Alba'
4. 3 *Verbena* 'Sissinghurst'
5. 4 *Antirrhinum* (seed-raised mixture)

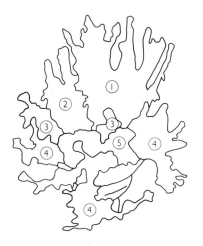

Page 64	Photographed 8 July

GROUP PLANTING
Permanent plantings of small shrubs, trained or 'poodled' as standards, and herbaceous perennials.
Position open and sunny

CONTAINERS A, B, C
Type terracotta azalea pots
Size height 6 inches, width 10 inches
Age 3 years

CONTAINER D
Type terracotta azalea pot
Size height 8 inches, width 10 inches
Age 6 years

CONTAINER E
Type terracotta standard flowerpot
Size height 6 inches, width 8 inches
Age 3 years

Key to plants
1. 1 *Cuphea hyssopifolia* 'Alba' (trained as a standard)

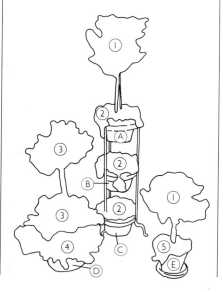

2. 5 per pot *Arabis ferdinandi-coburghii* 'Variegata'
3. 1 *Cuphea hyssopifolia* 'Alba' (trained as a standard and 'poodled' to form a basal ball shape)
4. 3 *Lobularia maritima* 'Minimum'
5. 1 *Veronica reptans*

Page 65	Photographed 8 July

CONTAINER
Type Italian terracotta rolled-rim pot, painted white
Size height 22 inches, width 26 inches
Age 10 years

PLANTING
A wire basket raised above the main container gives two tiers to this display of tender annual and perennial plants, and young shrubs grown for their foliage.
Position sheltered by nearby conifers

Key to plants
1. 3 *Impatiens* 'Actaea' (New Guinea hybrid)
2. 3 *Pelargonium* 'Sugar Baby'
3. 1 *Nierembergia caerulea* 'Lilac'
4. 3 *Pyracantha coccinea* 'Variegata'
5. 3 *Impatiens* 'Actaea' (New Guinea hybrid)
6. 1 *Nierembergia caerulea* 'Lilac'
7. *Coreopsis lanceolata* 'Sunray' (in border)

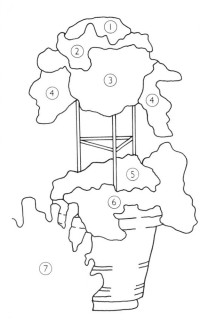

Page 66	Photographed 8 July

CONTAINER
Type petrified tree trunk
Size length 24 inches, width 18 inches
Age c. 65 million years!

PLANTING
A small summer display surrounded by permanent shrubs and herbaceous plants.
Position protected by other plants

Key to plants

1. 1 *Antirrhinum majus* 'Tahiti' (in 'log')
2. 1 *Lysimachia japonica* 'Minutissima' (in 'log')
3. 5 *Thymus serphyllum* 'Elfin' (in border)
4. 2 *Sempervivum tectorum* (in border)
5. 1 *Lysimachia nummularia* 'Aurea' (in border)
6. 1 *Picea abies* 'Nidiformis' (in border)
7. 1 *Pieris japonica* 'Compacta Variegata' (in border)
8. *Antirrhinum majus* cvs. (in border)
9. 3 *Arabis ferdinandi-coburgii* 'Variegata' (in border)
10. 1 *Cupressus sempervirens* 'Swane's Golden' (in border)
11. 1 *Zinnia linearis* (in border)
12. 1 *Oenothera fruticosa* (in border)

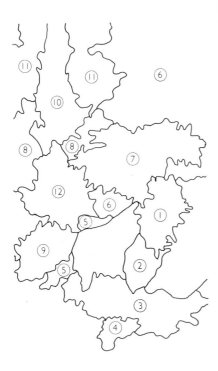

Page 67	Photographed 8 July

GROUP PLANTING

A collection of pots some planted permanently, others filled with summer colour.
Position sunny
Please note: the containers are described from left to right.

CONTAINER A

Type terracotta azalea pot
Size height 10 inches, width 20 inches
Age 3 years

Planting permanent evergreens and herbs

Key to plants

1. 2 *Hedera helix* 'Golden Ingot'
2. 1 *Impatiens walleriana* 'Peach Ice' (not yet in flower)
3. 1 *Origanum vulgare* 'Aureum Crispum'

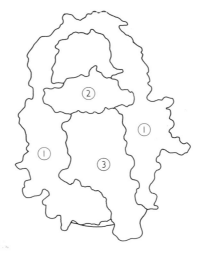

CONTAINER B

Type terracotta azalea pot
Size height 12 inches, width 14 inches
Age 5 years

Planting summer display

CONTAINER C

Type French terracotta flowerpot
Size height 6 inches, width 4 inches
Age 20 years

Planting permanent

Key to plants

1. 1 *Hibiscus acetocella* 'Red Shield'
2. 2 *Acorus gramineus* 'Ogon'
3. 1 *Veronica reptans*
4. 6 *Allium senescens*
5. 1 *Heuchera micrantha* 'Palace Purple'
6. 1 *Cuphea hyssopifolia*

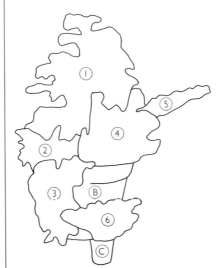

CONTAINER D

Type Malaysian glazed urn
Size height 10 inches, width 14 inches
Age 5 years

Planting permanent

Key to plants

1. 1 *Euonymus japonicus* 'Microphyllus'
2. 2 *Acorus gramineus* 'Ogon'
3. 1 *Veronica reptans*

CONTAINER E

Type Italian terracotta urn
Size height 10 inches, width 12 inches
Age 10 years

Planting summer display of hardy annuals and perennials

Key to plants

1. 1 *Coleus × hybridus* 'Volcano' (syn. *Solenostemon × hybridus* 'Volcano')
2. 1 *Impatiens* New Guinea hybrid
3. 1 *Lysimachia nummularia* 'Aurea'

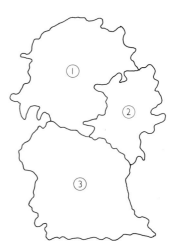

Page 69	Photographed 8 July

CONTAINER

Type Mexican terracotta open-mouthed pitcher
Size height 16 inches, width 18 inches
Age 5 years

PLANTING

A summer display of tender annual and perennial plants.
Position sheltered, west-facing

Key to plants

1. 3 *Zinnia linearis*
2. 1 *Verbena tenera*

3. *Verbena × hybrida* (in border)
4. *Iris ensata* 'Alba' (in border)

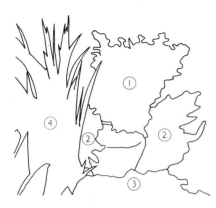

CONTAINER
Type copper kettle
Size height 24 inches, width 36 inches
Age 100 years or more

PLANTING
A semi-permanent display of decorative-leaved plants.
Position shaded and protected from cold winds

Key to plants
1. 1 *Sasaella masamuneana* 'Albostriata'
2. 1 *Arundinaria viridistriata* (syn. *Pleioblastus auricomus*)
3. 1 *Coleus × hybridus* 'Volcano' (syn. *Solenostemon × hybridus* 'Volcano')
4. 2 *Echinacea purpurea* 'Bravado'

THE ROYAL BOTANIC GARDENS
Mike Sinnott
Kew now has a policy not to use any peat in their cultivation of plants, whether in potting compost or in the preparation of soil for planting. Coir has proved to be an excellent peat-substitute. Pure coir compost is used for seed sowing, and for young plants which are potted-on or planted out after six to nine weeks. The urns and vases are filled with a mixture, made at Kew, of loam, coir and grit – at the rate of 25:30:15 respectively – and added nutrients.

The containers are fed once a fortnight with a liquid fertilizer, applied during a watering session.

CONTAINER
Type one of a pair of urns, possibly Coade stone
Size height 36 inches, width 36 inches
Age unknown

PLANTING
A summer display of purple-, silver- and glaucous-foliaged succulents, tender perennials and ornamental vegetables, planted in spring.
Position sunny and open, but with some protection afforded by surrounding trees

Key to plants
1. 1 large and 5 small *Aeonium arboreum* 'Atropurpureum'
2. 5 *Artemisia arborescens* 'Porquerolles'
3. 5 *Plectostachys serphyllifolia*
4. 25 palm cabbages (in border)
5. 200 'Hanako' and 'Yuka' ornamental kales (in border)
6. 200 'Bulls Blood' beetroots (in border)

CONTAINER
Type terracotta tazza
Size height 30 inches, width 35 inches
Age unknown

PLANTING
A summer display of annuals and tender perennials, planted in spring.
Position exposed to wind and rather cold

Key to plants
1. 1 *Heliotropium* 'Chatsworth'
2. 3 *Argyranthemum maderense*
3. 5 *Lobelia erinus* 'Emperor William'
4. 5 *Sanvitalia procumbens*

COTSWOLD SECLUSION
Mr and Mrs Smith
As the lead cisterns are no longer filled with water but with plants and the volume of compost needed for these large containers would be enormous, a more economical method of filling them is practised. Firstly a generous layer of drainage material is put in to cover the bottom, followed by enough soil from the vegetable garden to fill the cisterns to about eighteen inches below the rim. Then loam-based potting compost (John Innes No. 2) is used to top them up, and it is into this that the young plants are set to give them a good start. The same procedure is followed for the reconstituted stone urns, but the smaller lead vases are filled only with loam-based potting compost over a shallow layer of drainage material.

A liquid feed is applied to all containers from June to September.

CONTAINER
Type lead cistern
Size height 30 inches, width 18 inches, length 35 inches
Age 1797

PLANTING
A display of tender perennials and shrubs, planted in spring.
Position west-facing wall

Key to plants
1. 3 *Agyranthemum gracile*
2. 1 *Alyogyne huegelii* 'Santa Cruz'
3. 2 *Verbena* 'Loveliness'
4. 1 *Lobelia richardsonii*
5. 2 *Osteospermum* 'Brickell's Hybrid'

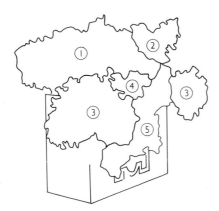

Pages 82–83	*Photographed 26 June*

CONTAINER
Type reconstituted stone urns
Size height 31 inches, width 25 inches
Age twentieth century

PLANTING
A display of tender perennials planted in spring.
Position exposed, but with some shelter from the east

Key to plants
1. 1 *Fuchsia* 'Thalia'
2. 2 *Verbena* 'Kemerton'
3. 2 *Verbena* 'Sissinghurst'
4. 3 *Diascia* 'Ruby Field'

SUNNYSIDE FARM
Jim Keeling

A large number of pots, some eighty or ninety of different shapes and sizes, are planted every year in early April, using a loam-based compost (John Innes No. 3). These are the pots to be taken to the Chelsea Flower Show in late May. After planting, the pots are crammed into a polythene tunnel where they are forced into growth with the help of the increasing day length, the warmth of the sun and liquid feeding every other day; the aim is to have them flowering by mid-May.

After Chelsea, feeding is reduced to once a week using a proprietary powder concentrate liquid feed. Jim also uses a special homemade 'brew' – a dilute solution of sheep drag or droppings, the concentrate of which is kept in a large barrel.

Page 84	*Photographed 27 June*

CONTAINER
Type terracotta Ali Baba pot decorated with handles
Size height 31 inches, width 22 inches
Age new

PLANTING
A mixture of summer-flowering tender perennials planted in spring. (Also shown on front cover.)
Position west-facing

Key to plants
1. 2 *Scaevola aemula* 'Blue Fan'
2. 2 *Verbena* 'Linda'
3. 1 *Diascia rigescens*
4. 2 *Diascia* 'Ruby Field'
5. 2 *Solenopsis auxillaris*
6. 3 *Verbena tenuisecta*

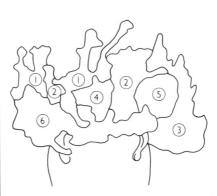

Page 87	*Photographed 27 June*

CONTAINER
Type terracotta pastry pot
Size height 19 inches, width 26 inches
Age 2 years

PLANTING
A single-colour display of tender perennials planted in spring.
Position west-facing

Key to plants
1. 4 *Pelargonium* 'Crimson Unique'
2. 2 *Verbena* 'Lawrence Johnson'

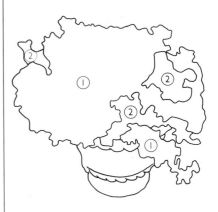

Page 88	*Photographed 27 June*

CONTAINER
Type orange pot
Size height 19 inches, width 26 inches
Age new

PLANTING
Permanently planted evergreens for display throughout the year.
Position against a south-facing wall

Key to plants
1. 1 *Ligustrum ovalifolium* 'Aureum' (trained as a standard)
2. 1 *Hedera helix* 'Nymans'
3. 5 *Hedera helix* 'Ivalace'
4. *Stachys byzantina* 'Sheila McQueen' (in border)
5. *Origanum laevigatum* (in border)
6. *Lavandula angustifolia* (in border)

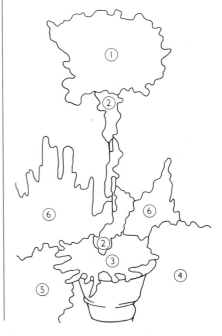

CONTAINER
Type   terracotta wall pot
Size   10 inches, width 10 inches
Age   3 years

PLANTING
A summer-flowering mixture of tender perennials planted in spring.
Position   west-facing timber-clad wall

Key to plants
1. 2 *Verbena* 'Linda'
2. 1 *Scaevola aemula* 'Blue Fan'
3. 1 *Felicia amelloides* 'Santa Anita'
4. 2 *Lobelia erinus compacta* 'Crystal Palace'

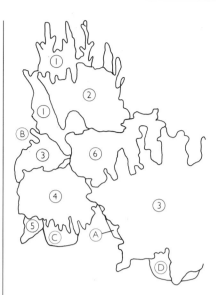

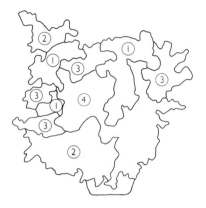

GROUP PLANTING
A display of pots planted with a mixture of tender perennials, sub-shrubs and annuals in strong shades of pink, red and purple.
Position   north-facing wall

CONTAINER A
Type   terracotta Ali Baba pot
Size   height 20 inches, width 17 inches
Age   new

CONTAINER B
Type   terracotta lily pot
Size   height 22 inches, width 30 inches
Age   new

CONTAINER C
Type   terracotta pastry pot
Size   height 13 inches, width 19 inches
Age   1 year

CONTAINER D
Type   terracotta orange pot
Size   height 19 inches, width 26 inches
Age   1 year

Key to plants
1. 5 *Atriplex hortensis* 'Rubra'
2. 3 *Lychnis coronaria*
3. 3 *Verbena* 'Kemerton'
4. 1 *Salvia officinalis* 'Purpurascens'
5. 2 *Viola labradorica*
6. 1 *Fuchsia* 'Violet Gem'

CONTAINER E
Type   terracotta wall pot
Size   height 10 inches, width 10 inches
Age   3 years

Key to plants
1. 2 *Verbena* 'Linda'
2. 1 *Scaevola aemula* 'Blue Fan'
3. 1 *Verbena tenuisecta*
4. 2 *Lobelia erinus compacta* 'Crystal Palace'
5. 1 *Felicia amelloides* 'Santa Anita'

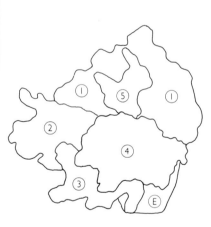

CONTAINER
Type   terracotta pan with basketwork decoration
Size   height 8 inches, width 20 inches
Age   1 year

PLANTING
A combination of herbs and summer-flowering tender perennials.
Position   against a south-facing wall

Key to plants
1. 1 *Salvia officinalis* 'Purpurascens'
2. 5 *Brachycome multifida*
3. 4 *Diascia* 'Ruby Field'

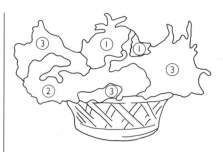

THE HALL AND THE VICARAGE
Myles Hildyard and Isabella Hildyard
Michael Blagg, head gardener at the Hall, makes up his own peat-free compost. Leafmould dug from the woods acts as a peat substitute, and this is mixed with horticultural sand and loamy soil from the vegetable garden.

The farm manager supplies Michael with a high potash fertilizer (the same used for the winter wheat crop). This is mixed into the compost and sustains the plants throughout summer without the need for additional feeding – liquid or otherwise.

CONTAINER
Type   English cast-iron urn with handles
Size   height 31 inches, width 21 inches
Age   Victorian

PLANTING
A display of flowering tender perennials planted in spring.
Position   a shady courtyard sheltered from the wind

Key to plants
1. 3 *Pelargonium* 'Decora Lilas'
2. 2 *Pelargonium* 'Decora Rouge'
3. 2 *Pelargonium* PELFI Sofie
4. 3 *Lobelia erinus compacta* 'Cambridge Blue'

CONTAINER
Type classic campana vase
Size height 24 inches, width 19 inches
Age originals 1853, but some modern

PLANTING
A summer display planted in spring.
Position sunny but exposed

Plants 3 *Pelargonium* 'Henderinum' and 3 *Lobelia erinus compacta* 'Cambridge Blue'

CONTAINER
Type terracotta pastry pot
Size height 17 inches, width 24 inches
Age new

PLANTING
A colourful mixture of herbs, ornamental vegetables and flowers for summer display.
Position southeast corner

Key to plants
1. 1 *Aloysia triphylla*
2. 1 *Salvia officinalis*
3. 1 *Mentha suaveolens* 'Variegata'
4. 1 *Nicotiana* Domino series
5. 1 *Ocimum basilicum* 'Dark Opal' (basil)
6. 1 *Brassica oleracea* white form
7. 1 *Tropaeolum majus* 'Alaska'
8. 1 *Brassica oleracea* purple form
9. 1 *Petroselinum crispum* (parsley)
10. *Stachys byzantina* (in border)

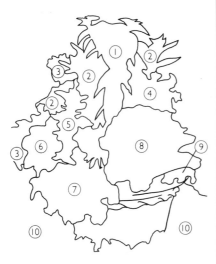

WHITE BARN HOUSE
Beth Chatto
Compost is bought in bulk for the many thousands of plants produced on the nursery. The peat-based medium has extra grit incorporated to improve the drainage and, to keep the compost more open and, for purposes of economy, some rotted garden compost is also

added. A slow-release fertilizer, effective over a nine-month period, is also mixed in. The pots are refilled with fresh compost every spring. After planting a supplementary top-dressing of quick-acting fertilizer is added to give plants an initial boost.

GROUP PLANTING
A collection of traditional English terracotta flowerpots planted with succulents and tender perennials for summer display.
Summer position sheltered, southeast-facing
Winter position in a frost-free glasshouse

Key to plants and pots (height × width)
1. 1 *Agave americana* 'Marginata' 12 × 12 inches
2. 1 *Pelargonium* 'Decora Rouge'
3. 2 *Pelargonium* 'Decora Lilas'
4. 2 *Helichrysum petiolare* 19 × 17 inches
5. 2 *Argyranthemum gracile* 9 × 12 inches
6. 2 *Pelargonium* 'Decora Lilas'
7. 2 *Verbena* 'Silver Anne' 12 × 13 inches
8. 1 *Graptopetalum paraguayense* 5 × 8 inches
9. 1 *Hippeastrum* 'Fire Dance' 8 × 6 inches
10. 1 *Echeveria* c.f. *gilva* 8 × 9 inches
11. 1 *Senecio* species 5 × 7 inches

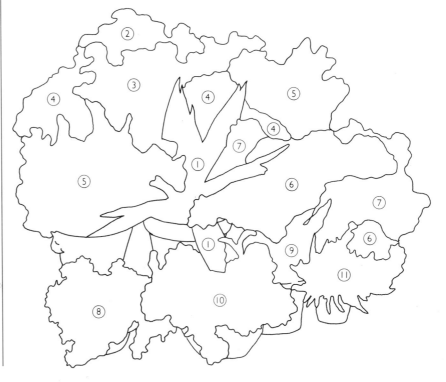

CONTAINER
Type Spanish terracotta Ali Baba pot with handles
Size height 12 inches, width 9 inches
Age 10 years

PLANTING
A combination of tender perennials for flower and foliage planted in spring.
Position sheltered, south-facing

Key to plants
1. 1 *Argyranthemum* 'Blizzard'
2. *Pelargonium* 'Burton's Variety' (in border)
3. *Helichrysum petiolare* (in border)

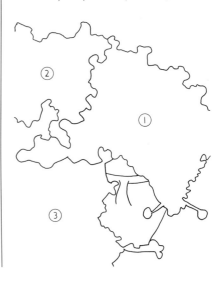

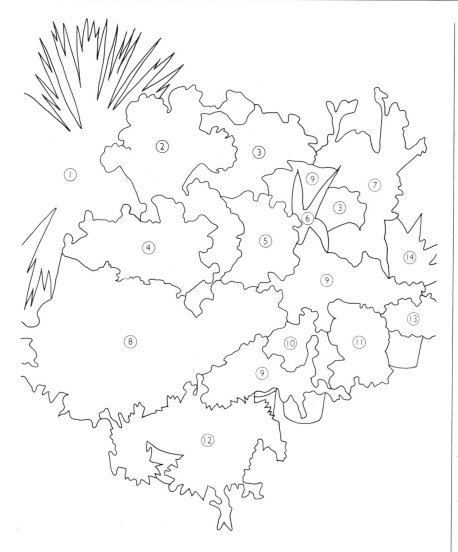

Summer position east-facing
Winter position in a frost-free glasshouse

Plants 1 *Agave americana* 'Marginata' and 2 *Lotus berthelotii*

Page 105	Photographed 31 July

GROUP PLANTING
Massed shrubs, tender perennials, annuals and grasses planted individually in pots of plastic, fibre and traditional English terracotta.
Position west-facing

Key to plants
1. 3 *Arundo donax* 'Variegata'
2. 1 *Hydrangea macrocarpa* cv.
3. 1 *Fuchsia* cv.
4. 2 *Nicotiana langsdorfii*
5. 1 *Lotus berthelotii*
6. 3 *Petunia* × *hybrida* Resisto series
7. 2 *Fuchsia* cv.
8. 1 *Helichrysum petiolare* 'Variegatum'
9. 1 *Aeonium manriqueorum*

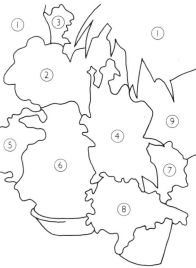

RODMARTON MANOR
Simon and Christina Biddulph
The containers on the terraces at Rodmarton are rather large to be filled with bought compost. So after a layer of broken Cotswold slates and small stones have covered the bottom of a container to a depth of at least three inches, a layer of soil from the kitchen garden is added. This is capped with eighteen inches of good loam-based potting compost. In the 'troughery' the stone troughs are filled with a very free-draining mixture, high in coarse grit. The pots are top-dressed in summer with an organic fertilizer of blood, fish and bone. In addition the plants are liquid-fed weekly with a diluted powder-base fertilizer.

Page 103	Photographed 31 July

GROUP PLANTING
A collection of traditional English terracotta flowerpots filled with tender plants and succulents. These flower pots are planted up and grouped together in spring eventually to to form a summer 'border' as the massed growth obscures the pots.
Position south-facing

Key to plants and pots (height × width)
1. 1 *Cordyline australis*
   12 × 14 inches
2. 1 *Aeonium arboreum* 'Atropurpureum'
   9 × 14 inches
3. 2 *Pelargonium* 'Decora Lilas'
   18 × 14 inches
4. 1 *Argyranthemum* 'Blizzard'
   12 × 12 inches
5. 1 *Pelargonium* 'Frank Headley'
   12 × 12 inches
6. 1 *Agave americana* 'Marginata'
   10 × 10 inches
7. 1 *Nicotiana langsdorfii*
   6 × 8 inches

8. 2 *Verbena* 'Silver Anne'
   12 × 12 inches
9. 1 *Helichrysum petiolare*
   7 × 8 inches
10. 1 *Argyranthemum maderense*
    6 × 8 inches
11. 4 *Echeveria* c.f. *gilva*
    7 × 13 inches
12. 3 *Dudleya farinosa*
    5 × 10 inches
13. *Pelargonium* 'Vancounver Centennial'
    6 × 8 inches
14. *Agave americana*
    10 × 10 inches

Page 104	Photographed 31 July

CONTAINER
Type Spanish terracotta terrace pot
Size height 16 inches, width 19 inches
Age 3 years
PLANTING
A permanent specimen succulent with tender trailing plants.

GROUP PLANTING

Pre-1900 troughs planted permanently with alpines, one of each type.
Position open, gaining maximum light

CONTAINER A

Type Cotswold-stone trough
Size height 11 inches, width and depth 30 inches

Plants
Achillea × kolbiana
Dianthus 'Icomb'
Dianthus 'Whitehills'
Erodium daucoides
Geranium cinereum
Oxalis adenophylla
Phlox 'Kelly's Eye'
Phlox subulata 'Amazing Grace'
Saxifraga 'Maria Luisa'
Silene schafta
Thymus praecox 'Porlock'

CONTAINER B

Type wooden trough
Size height 12 inches, width 23 inches, length 33 inches

Plants
Alyssum saxatile 'Compactum'
Dryas octopetala 'Minor'
Erodium glandulosum
Erodium reichardii
Gypsophila repens 'Dorothy Teacher'
Gypsophila repens 'Rosea'
Papaver alpinum album
Veronica prostrata

CONTAINER C

Type Cotswold-stone trough
Size height 10 inches, width 16 inches, length 26 inches

Plants
Narcissus asturiensis
Narcissus 'Cedric Morris'
Narcissus 'Little Beauty'
Polygonum vaccinifolium
Pulsatilla campanella
Pulsatilla halleri
Pulsatilla vernalis
Pulsatilla vulgaris rubra
Thymus × citriodorus 'Bertram Anderson'

CONTAINER D

Type Cotswold-stone trough
Size height 7 inches, width 24 inches, length 53 inches

Plants
Cotoneaster congestus nanus
Dianthus deltoides
Erinus alpinus
Hebe cupressoides 'Boughton Dome'
Juniperus communis 'Compressa'
Phlox subulata 'Scarlet Flame'
Primula marginata 'Linda Pope'
Thymus 'Doone Valley'
Tulipa linifolia Batalinii Group
Veronica saturejoides

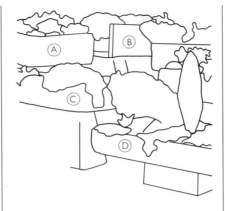

CONTAINER A

Type reconstituted stone urn
Size height 24 inches, width 38 inches
Age pre-1960

CONTAINER B

Type reconstituted stone urn
Size height 22 inches, width 24 inches
Age pre-1960

PLANTING

A summer display of tender shrubs and perennials planted in late spring.
Position sheltered, south-facing terrace backed by the house

Key to plants
1. 5 *Fuchsia* 'Rose of Denmark'
2. 5 *Pelargonium* 'Mrs E.G. Hill'

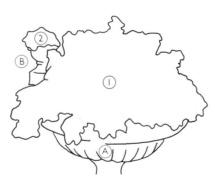

GROUP PLANTING

A collection of large containers planted with tender perennials, some permanently, others for summer display.
Position hot and sheltered, south-facing terrace. The agapanthus are housed under glass for the winter

CONTAINER A

Type plastic silage chemical container cut in half
Size height 19 inches, width 24 inches
Age 5 years

CONTAINER B

Type elm box, painted white
Size height 25 inches, width 30 inches, depth 30 inches
Age 15 years

CONTAINER C

Type reconstituted stone vase with draped decoration
Size height 24 inches, width 30 inches
Age pre-1970

Key to plants
1. 3 *Agapanthus africanus*
2. 3 *Argyranthemum foeniculaceum*
3. 1 *Pelargonium* 'Lady Plymouth'

CONTAINER

Type simple concrete dish
Size height 14 inches, width 35 inches
Age pre-1975

PLANTING

A summer display of tender perennials and shrubs for flower and foliage planted in spring.
Position southwest corner of garden

Key to plants
1. 1 *Abutilon pictum* 'Thompsonii'
2. 2 *Fuchsia magellanica* 'Versicolor'

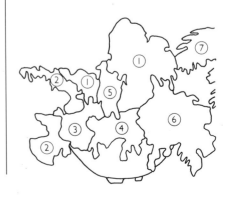

3. I *Pelargonium* 'Hederinum'
4. I *Fuchsia* 'Rose of Denmark'
5. I *Fuchsia* cv.
6. I *Fuchsia* 'Achievement'
7. I *Leycesteria formosa* (in border)

| Page III | Photographed 10 June |

CONTAINER A

Type stone drinking trough
Size height 12 inches, width 25 inches, depth 21 inches
Age pre-1850

PLANTING

A permanent planting of alpines growing closely together.
Position open, gaining maximum light

Key to plants

1. 2 *Campanula garganica* 'Blue Diamond'
2. 3 *Helianthemum* 'Double Apricot' and 3 *Helianthemum* 'Ben Afflick'

CONTAINER B

Type stone urn
Size height 18 inches, width 16 inches
Age pre-1960

PLANTING

One of a pair of urns placed on gate piers, each of which is planted with hardy herbaceous perennials.
Position exposed, south-facing

Plants 3 *Campanula carpatica* 'Chewton Joy'

HIGH VICTORIAN STYLE
Susan Dickinson

When new or when taken out after winter storage, the large terracotta pots used in the garden are immersed in the vinery rainwater tanks for twenty-four hours to absorb moisture. This prevents the porous terracotta from robbing the compost of water.

Young plants, large enough to handle, are potted individually into four-inch pots filled with pure cocofibre in which they grow away quickly. To wean the plants off this very fibrous compost,

the large decorative containers used in the garden are filled with a mixture of two-thirds loam-based compost, of John Innes No. 2 composition, to one third cocofibre.

It has been found that cocofibre compost tends to lose its nutrients rather more quickly than its peat- or loam-based equivalent, so frequent liquid feeding is important. Daturas and sparmannias are fed with a high nitrogen liquid fertilizer every day. *Pelargonium tomentosum* grown for its foliage, heliotropes and lemon verbena are fed weekly, also with a high nitrogen fertilizer. All other pots have a balanced liquid feed applied once a week until feeding ceases in mid-September.

| Pages 114–115 | Photographed 17 July |

CONTAINERS

Type Italiante terracotta pots
Size height 22 inches, width 30 inches
Age 2 years

PLANTING

A summer display of half-hardy plants and tender perennials in pots and in the border.
Position northwest-facing, sheltered by the house and nearby trees

Key to plants

1. I *Cordyline australis* 'Atropurpurea'
2. 2 *Salvia fulgens*
3. 6 *Nicotiana affinis* 'Lime Green' (also in border)
4. 2 *Fuchsia* 'Chang'

5. 2 *Pelargonium* 'Paul Crampel' (also in border)
6. 2 *Hosta* 'Royal Standard' (also in border)
7. 2 *Pelargonium* 'Yale'
8. *Dahlia* 'Bishop of Llandaff' (in border)
9. *Cordyline indivisa* (in border)

| Page 117 | Photographed 17 July |

CONTAINER

Type white marble tazza
Size height 18 inches, width 22 inches
Age nineteenth century

PLANTING

A summer display of half-hardy plants.
Position southwest-facing

Key to plants

1. I *Yucca gloriosa* 'Variegata'
2. 6 *Petunia* light blue-flowered F_1 hybrid
3. 2 *Pelargonium* 'L'Elegante'

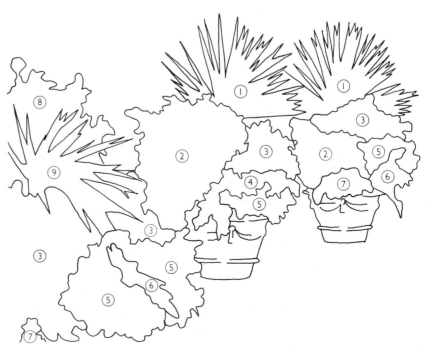

CONTAINER
Type terracotta flowerpot
Size height 15 inches, width 21 inches
Age 1 year

PLANTING
A tender shrub permanently planted for summer display outdoors.
Summer position southeast-facing
Winter position frost-free glasshouse

Key to plants
1. 1 *Datura cornigera* 'Knightii' (syn. *Brugmansia cornigera* 'Knightii')
2. *Cobaea scandens* 'Alba'
3. *Ipomoea* 'Heavenly Blue' (in border)
4. *Nicotiana sylvestris* (in border)

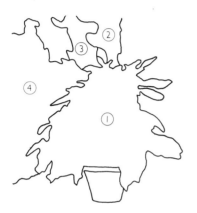

CONTAINER
Type dark brown plastic tub
Size height 14 inches, width 24 inches
Age new

PLANTING
A mixture of tender annuals and perennials planted in spring for summer display.
Position sheltered, sun or partial shade

Key to plants
1. 2 *Argyranthemum* 'Jamaica Primrose'
2. 1 *Osteospermum* 'Whirligig'
3. 6 *Petunia* white-flowered F₁ hybrid
4. 2 *Bidens ferulifolia*
5. 3 *Helichrysum petiolare* 'Limelight'

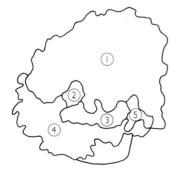

GROUP PLANTING
A group of pots planted with tender perennials and half-hardy plants, in shades of red and purple, planted in spring.
Position south-facing

CONTAINER A
Type terracotta pot decorated with basketwork
Size height 8 inches, width 12 inches
Age 1 year

CONTAINER B
Type English terracotta flowerpot
Size height 8 inches, width 9 inches
Age modern

CONTAINER C
Type English terracotta flowerpot
Size height 9 inches, width 10 inches
Age pre-1920

Key to plants
1. 1 *Heliotropium* 'Princess Marina'
2. 1 *Pelargonium* 'Paul Crampel'
3. 1 *Pelargonium* 'Double Jacoby'
4. 1 *Pelargonium* 'Caroline Schmidt'
5. 1 *Senecio bicolor cineraria* 'Cirrus'
6. 1 *Pelargonium* 'Rambler Supreme'
7. 1 *Pelargonium* 'Paul Crampel'
8. 1 *Origanum laevigatum* 'Hopley's'
9. 1 *Salvia fulgens*
10. 1 *Pericallis lanata*
11. 1 *Plectostachys serphyllifolia*

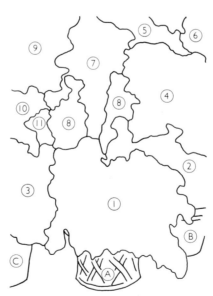

CONNECTICUT COLOR
Gary Keim
Gary uses a proprietary soil-less compost, a mixture of peat and perlite, in his many pots. Due to the large number of pots involved, he find this easier than mixing his own and the results have always been good. By incorporating water-absorbing polymers into the compost, longer intervals can be left between waterings than with ordinary mixes. He believes strongly in careful and regular feeding throughout the growing season. The containers are fed once a fortnight using a balanced fertilizer (NPK 20:20:20). At times, especially toward the end of summer, he applies a liquid feed (NPK 10:30:20) to promote a late flush of bloom.

CONTAINER
Type concrete planter with river-stone border
Size height 44 inches (including pedestal), width 19 inches
Age early twentieth century

PLANTING
A summer display of pansies.
Position open and sunny

Plants 6 *Viola* 'Jolly Joker' (violet and orange bicolour) and 6 *V.* 'Spanish Sun' (orange and yellow bicolour)

CONTAINER
Type terracotta flowerpot
Size height 12 inches, width 13 inches
Age 3 years

PLANTING
A summer display of tender perennials.
Position full sun

Key to plants
1. 2 *Verbena canadensis* 'Homestead Purple'
2. 1 *Convolvulus sabatius*
3. 1 *Canna* 'Pretoria' (in border)

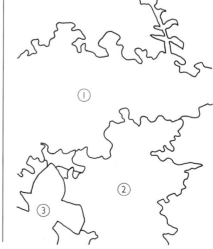

GROUP PLANTING

A group of pots planted with tender perennials and pansies for summer display.
Position   open and sunny

CONTAINERS A, B
Type   terracotta pot
Size   height 13 inches, width 12 inches
Age   1 year

CONTAINERS C
Type   cast stoneware Celtic planter
Size   height 6 inches, width 9 inches
Age   2 years

Key to plants
1.   3 *Petunia* 'Azure Pearls'
2.   3 *Verbena* 'Sissinghurst'
3.   3 *Viola* (to match *Petunia* 'Azure Pearls')
4.   *Nicotiana alata* 'Grandiflora' (in border)
5.   *Lilium* 'Ming Yellow' (in border)

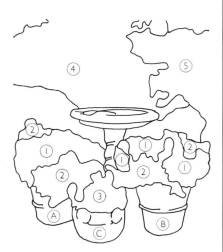

GROUP PLANTING

A varied but harmonious collection of specimen plants in terracotta flowerpots.
Position   sunny, within a sheltered garden

Key to plants and pots (height × width)
1.   1 *Gazania* 'Cookei'
     $6\frac{1}{2}$ × 8 inches
2.   1 *Phormium* 'Sundowner'
     $7\frac{1}{2}$ × $7\frac{1}{2}$ inches
3.   Universal pansies (red and yellow mixture)
     $8\frac{1}{2}$ × 9 inches
4.   1 *Euonymus fortunei* 'Emerald 'n' Gold'
     6 × 8 inches
5.   1 *Phormium* 'Yellow Wave'
     6 × $6\frac{1}{2}$ inches
6.   1 *Corokia cotoneaster*
     $8\frac{1}{2}$ × 8 inches
7.   1 *Carex buchananii*
     $6\frac{1}{2}$ × $6\frac{1}{2}$ inches
8.   1 *Pelargonium* 'Lady Cullum'
     $8\frac{1}{2}$ × 9 inches

9.   1 *Phormium cookianum hookeri* 'Tricolor'
     7 × 8 inches
10.   1 *Phormium* 'Sundowner'
     $7\frac{1}{2}$ × $7\frac{1}{2}$ inches
11.   1 *Plectranthus* 'Aureus'
     5 × 8 inches
12.   1 *Phormium cookianum hookeri* 'Tricolor'
     7 × 8 inches
13.   1 *Pelargonium* 'Crystal Palace Gem'
     $8\frac{1}{2}$ × 9 inches
14.   1 *Verbascum undulatum*
     $6\frac{1}{2}$ × $6\frac{1}{2}$ inches
15.   1 *Viola* 'Roc Red'
     $8\frac{1}{2}$ × 9 inches
16.   1 *Carex flagellifera*
     6 × $7\frac{1}{2}$ inches
17.   1 *Cupressus macrocarpa* 'Goldcrest'
     $6\frac{1}{2}$ × 6 inches

CONTAINER
Type   terracotta flowerpot
Size   height 10 inches, width 14 inches
Age   4 years

PLANTING
A summer display of tender plants.
Position   sunny and open, but protected by nearby trees

Key to plants
1.   1 *Cordyline australis*
2.   3 *Petunia integrifolia* var. *integrifolia*

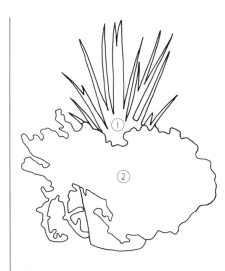

SOUTHVIEW
Rupert Golby

Ever since the revelations concerning the exploitation of peat bogs I have switched to using a 50:50 mixture of loam-based potting compost (John Innes No. 3) and multipurpose cocofibre composts. The plants have responded well, making excellent root growth. I liquid feed twice a week, alternating between a liquid foliar feed, and powder concentrate which is taken up by the roots. Winter-planted pots are not fed.

Page 2 — *Photographed 20 September*

CONTAINER
Type cylindrical lead pot
Size height 11 inches, width 13 inches
Age nineteenth century

PLANTING
A semi-permanent display of dwarf shrubs and a herbaceous perennial climber.
Position low south-facing wall, backed by a box hedge giving shelter from the north

Key to plants
1. 1 *Berberis thunbergii* 'Harlequin'
2. 3 *Hebe pinguifolia* 'Pagei'
3. 3 *Convolvulus elegantissimus*
4. 1 *Salvia officinalis* 'Purpurascens'

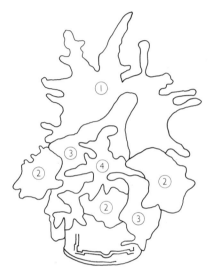

Page 126 — *Photographed 18 February*

CONTAINER
Type stone horseshoe-shaped trough
Size height 10 inches, width 28 inches
Age early nineteenth century

PLANTING
A winter planting of bulbs and overwintering rosettes of biennials. Planted in October for midwinter display.
Position shady courtyard

Key to plants
1. 100 *Galanthus nivalis*
2. 9 *Glaucium flavum*

Page 129 — *Photographed 18 February*

CONTAINER
Type hot water copper made of copper
Size height 16 inches, width 22 inches
Age Victorian

PLANTING
A winter display of evergreens with the deciduous oso berry. A fine garrya planted in the border provides the backdrop.
Position a cold sunless corner facing north-east.

Key to plants
1. 1 *Oemleria cerasiformis* (syn. *Osmaronia cerasiformis*)
2. 5 *Helleborus foetidus*
3. 1 *Hedera helix* 'Poetica' and 1 *H. azorica*
4. 1 *Garrya elliptica* 'James Roof' (in border)

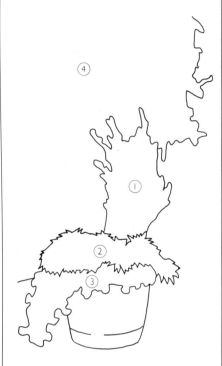

Pages 130 — *Photographed 7 March*

CONTAINER
Type terracotta urn from Impruneta
Size height 22 inches, width 19 inches
Age 10 years

PLANTING
A semi-permanent planting of rich colours for winter and spring interest set against a large winter-flowering shrub.
Position in the open within a walled garden.

Key to plants
1. 1 *Photinia × fraseri* 'Red Robin'
2. 1 *Skimmia japonica* 'Rubella' (a male cultivar)
3. 1 *Epimedium × rubrum*
4. 1 *Hedera helix* (wild seedling)
5. 1 *Viburnum × bodnantense* 'Dawn'

Page 131 — *Photographed 18 February*

CONTAINER
Type hot-water copper, made of copper
Size height 24 inches, width 36 inches
Age Victorian

PLANTING
A permanently planted selection of evergreens with an ornamental willow for late-winter interest.
Position in a south-west corner

Key to plants
1. 1 *Salix caprea* 'Kilmarnock'
2. 1 *Hedera helix* 'Nymans'
3. 2 *Prunus laurocerasus* 'Otto Luyken'
4. 2 *Helleborus argutifolius*
5. 3 *Hedera helix* 'Persian Carpet'
6. 4 *Helleborus foetidus*
7. 1 *Hebe rakaiensis*
8. 15 *Arum italicum pictum*

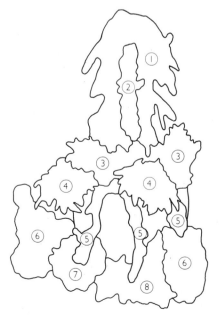

Page 132   *Photographed 18 February*

CONTAINER

Type terracotta box from Impruneta
Size height 16 inches, width and depth 21 inches
Age 10 years

PLANTING

A permanent planting of box balls, clipped to shape.
Position against a west-facing wall

Key to plants

1. 9 *Buxus sempervirens*
2. 3 *Hedera helix* 'Chicago'

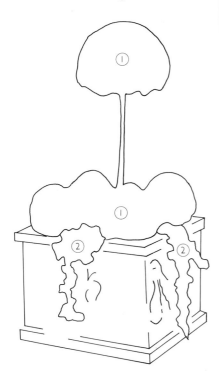

Page 132–33   *Photographed 18 February*

CONTAINER

Type small stone horseshoe-shaped trough
Size height 7 inches, width 19 inches
Age early nineteenth century

PLANTING

A permanent planting with the dramatic black foliage of *Ophiopogon*, enlivened in late winter by crocuses.
Position against a south-facing stone bench

Key to plants

1. 25 *Crocus tommasinianus* 'Whitewell Purple'
2. 9 *Ophiopogon planiscarpus nigrescens*
3. *Helleborus foetidus* (in border)
4. *Mahonia aquifolium* 'Apollo' (in border)
5. *Bergenia cordifolia* 'Purpurea' (in border)
6. *Ajuga reptans* 'Atropurpurea' (in border)
7. *Koeleria glauca* (in border)
8. *Crocus tommasinianus* (in border)

Page 134   *Photographed 18 February*

CONTAINER

Type terracotta pot decorated with nectarines
Size height 8 inches, width 13 inches
Age new

PLANTING

An early-spring planting of white flowers.
Position against a northeast-facing wall

Key to plants

1. 3 *Helleborus orientalis* (white-flowered hybrids)
2. 30 *Crocus chrysanthus* 'Snow Bunting'
3. 5 *Hedera helix* 'Sagittifolia Variegata'

Page 135   *Photographed 22 December*

CONTAINER

Type oval terracotta basket with handles
Size height 7 inches, width 15 inches
Age new, but aged with a lime wash

PLANTING

An indoor Christmas display planted in early November.
Position the hearth of a well-lit room

Key to plants

1. 18 *Narcissus papyraceus* (N. 'Paper White')
2. twigs of *Salix matsudana* 'Tortuosa'
3. 9 *Soleirolia soleirolii* 'Silver Queen' (syn. *Helxine soleirolia*)

Back jacket   *Photographed 18 February*

CONTAINER

Type terracotta trough from Impruneta
Size height 15 inches, width 10 inches, length 45 inches
Age 10 years

PLANTING

A permanent planting with bulbs.
Position against an east-facing wall

Plants 15 *Buxus sempervirens*, (box balls), 40 *Galanthus nivalis*, 1 *Hedera helix* 'Gracilis' and 1 *Milium effusum aureum*

FURTHER READING

—.*Classic Garden Design: How to Adapt and Recreate Garden Features of the Past.* New York: Random House, 1989.

—.*The Random House Book of Perennials.* New York: Random House, 1991.

Bloom, Alan. *Alpines for Your Garden.* Edited for U.S. Gardeners by Derek Fell. Chicago: Floraprint U.S.A., 1981.

Conran, Terence. *Terence Conran's Garden Style: Furnishing the Room Outside.* New York: Crown, 1991.

Griswold, Mac, and Weller, Eleanor. *The Golden Age of American Gardens.* New York: Harry N. Abrams, Inc., 1991.

Hobhouse, Penelope. *Colour in Your Garden.* New York: Little, Brown, 1985.

Hudak, Joseph. *Gardening with Perennials.* Portland: Timber Press, 1985.

Innes, Miranda. *The Ornamental Gardener: Creative Ideas for Every Garden.* Owings Mills: Stemmer House Publishers, 1992.

Jekyll, Gertrude. *Garden Ornament.* Wappinger's Falls, N.Y.: Antique Collectors' Club, 1984.

Koreshoff, Deborah R. *Bonsai: Its Art, Science, History and Philosophy.* Portland: Timber Press, 1985.

de L'estrieux, Elizabeth. *The Art of Gardening in Pots.* Wappinger's Falls, N.Y.: Antique Collectors' Club, 1991.

Plumptre, George. *Garden Ornament.* New York: Saga Press, 1990.

LIST OF SUPPLIERS

Please note: all names, addresses and telephone numbers were correct at the time this book went to press.

CONTAINERS

Classic Garden Ornaments, Ltd.
Longshadow Gardens
Pomona, IL 62975
(800) 852–2299
Whichford pottery; traditional garden ornaments.

French Wyres
P.O. Box 131655
Tyler, Texas 75713
(903) 597–8322
Urns, window boxes, plant stands, etc.

Kinsman Company, Inc.
River Road
Point Pleasant,
PA 18950
(800) 733–5613
Planters, plant stands, hanging baskets, etc.

Kenneth Lynch & Sons
84 Danbury Road
Wilton, CT 06897
(203) 762–8363
Classic containers, urns, etc.

Moultrie Manufacturing Co.
P.O. Box 1179
Moultrie, GA 31776
(912) 985–1312
Classical cast-aluminum urns.

Elizabeth Schumacher's Garden Accents
4 Union Hill Road
W. Conshohocken, PA 19428
(800) 296–5525
Containers, urns, garden ornaments.

Smith & Hawken
117 East Strawberry Drive
Mill Valley, CA 94941
(415) 389–8300
Whichford pottery, etc.

Thomas Woodworks
76 Arrowhead Drive
New Hartford, CT 06098
(800) 866–4866
Cedar, teak and mahogany planters.

PLANTS

Bluestone Perennials
7201 Middle Ridge
Madison, OH 44057
(216) 428–7535

Bundles of Bulbs
112 Greenspring Valley Road
Owings Mills, MD 21117
(410) 363–1371
Tulips and other bulbs.

Carroll Gardens
P.O. Box 310
Westminster,
MD 21158
(410) 876–7336
Perennials.

Doornbosch Bros.
6455 River Pkwy
Milwaukee, WI 53213
(414) 476–9632
Tulips and other bulbs.

Glasshouse Works
P.O. Box 97, Church Street
Stewart, OH 45778–0097
(614) 662–2142
Succulents, tropicals, hardies.

Goodwin Creek Gardens
P.O. Box 83-H
Williams, OR 97544
(503) 846–7357
Lavenders, scented geraniums, herbs.

The Green Escape
P.O. Box 1417
Palm Harbour, FL 34682
(813) 784–1132
Tropical and cold-hardy palms.

Hardy Roses for the North
Box 273H
Danville, WA 99121–0273
(800) 442–8122

Hatten's Nursery, Inc.
6401 Overlook Road
Mobile, AL 36608
(205) 342–0505
Bougainvillea.

Hortico, Inc.
723 Robson Road
Waterdown, ON L0R 2H1
Canada
(416) 689–6984
Antique, English and other roses.

Logee's Greenhouses
141 North Street
Danielson, CT 06239
(203) 774–8038
Clivias, tropicals.

Marion Gardens
P.O. Box 247
East Marion, NY 11939
(516) 477–1010
Herbs.

Matsu-Momiji Nursery
P.O. Box 11414
Philadelphia, PA 19111
(215) 722–6286
Bonsai, containers.

Nor' East Miniature Roses
P.O. Box 307
Rowley, MA 01969
(508) 948–7964

Siskiyou Rare Plant Nursery
2825 Cummings Road
Medford, OR 97501
(503) 772–6846

Stemmer House Ornamental Nurseries
2627 Caves Road
Owings Mills, MD 21117
(410) 363–3690
Boxwood, pre-bonsai, topiary.

TC Plant inc.
23255 N.W. Evergreen St.
Hillsboro, OR 97124-5810
(503) 640–9116
Japanese maples, bonsai, accent plants.

Andre Viette Farm & Nursery
Rte 1, Box 16
Fishersville, VA 22939
(703) 943–2315
Perennials.

Weiss Bros. Perennial Nursery
11690 Colfax Hwy
Grass Valley, CA 95945
(916) 273–5814

Wheeler Farm Gardens
171 Bartlett Street
Portland, OR 06480
(203) 342–2374
Balcony geraniums of Europe.

White Flower Farm
P.O. Box 50
Litchfield, CT 06759
(203) 496–9624
Perennials, containers.

Winterthur Museum Garden and Library
Winterthur, DE 19735
(800) 767–0500
Containers, plants, accessories.

INDEX

Please note: page numbers in *italic* indicate illustrations.

Abutilon 94, 108, *111*
Acacia 94
Acaena 114
Acorus 67
Aeonium 50, 75, 76
Agapanthus 108, *109*, 137
Agave 50, 101, *102*, 102, *104*, 137
Ali Baba pots *52*, *84*
Allium christophii 32
Aloysia (Lemon verbena) 26, 116
Alyssum 33
Amaryllis 34
annuals 63, 64
Antirrhinum *66*
Arabis 64, 66
Argyranthemum 37, 113
    'Blizzard' *100*
    foeniculaceum 53, *74*, 75
    'Jamaica Primrose' *119*
Artemisia 50, 75, 76
Arum italicum 131
Arundo donax 'Variegata' *105*
Augusta, Princess 75

Bamboos *136*
Banana 93
Barbarea 128
Barnsley, Ernest 107
Barnsley House 24, 25–6, *27–31*, 140–2
barrels *24*, 25, 26, *73*, 94
Basil *38*
basket pots 51
Bay 42–3, *44*
Beans 41, *46*
bedding plants *50*, 55
Beech 43
Beetroot 41, 75
Begonia 121
Berberis 26
    thunbergii 'Harlequin' *32*
Biddulph, Simon and Christina 107–8, 151–3
Blueberries 17
bog gardens 65, 86
Bougainvillea 17, 93
Box *see Buxus*
Brachycome multifida 72, *91*
brick containers 56
Brown, Lancelot 'Capability':
    park 41, *43*
Buddleja 64
bulbs *1*, 34, 51, 128
Burton, Decimus 72
Buxus (Box) *1*, 26, 27, *39*, 43, 51, *54*, 56, 64, 127–8, *132*

Cabbage 41, 75, 94
Camellia 34, 64, 93, *96*

Canna 75, 113
    'Assault' *74*
Carpenter, R C 79
Caryopteris 64
cast-iron containers 41, *47*, *92*
cattle trough *111*
cauldrons 41, *46*
ceramic pots 34
Chambers, Melanie 49–51, 143–4
Chambers, Sir William 75
Chatsworth *40*, 41–3, *42*, *43*–7, 142–3
Chatto, Beth 101–2, 150–1
Cherries *112*, 116
Cherubim 10–11
chimney pots 41
Chimonanthus 25
Christianity 9, 12
cisterns *48*, *80*
Citrus 17, *18*, 40, 42, 45, 59, 116
classic pot: making 7–13
clay pots 51
Clematis 55, 64
    'Gravetye Beauty' *36*
Cleome 26
Cobaea 26, 113, *118*
Coleus 136
compost 138
concrete containers 108
conifers: dwarf 65
Connecticut gardens *120*, 121–2, *122–5*, 154–5
conservatories 93
Convolvulus 60
    elegantissimus 2
    sabatius 122
copper containers 50, *129*, 137
Cordyline 102, 113, *114*, *125*
cornucopia 8–9
Cornus (Dogwood) 59, *61*, 128
Corylus avellana 'Contorta' 128
Cosmos 26
    atrosanguineus 51
Cotswold manor house *78*, 79–80, *80–3*, 147–8
Crab apple 64
creepers 56–9
Crocus 25, *31*, *132*
Cuphea hyssopifolia 64

Daffodil *see* Narcissus
Dahlia 113
Daisies 75, 128
Datura 31, 94, 114, *118*
death: plants connected with 11–12
Devonshire, Duchess of 41–3, 142–3
Dianthus 49
Diascia 26, *82*, *91*, 122
Dicentra 23
Dickinson, Susan 113–16, 153–4
Dogwood 59, *61*, 128
drainage 138

drinking troughs *106*

Echeveria 50
Elaeagnus 128
Elton Hall *54*, 55–9, *56–61*, 144–5
Euonymus 128
evergreens *56*, 64, 65

feeding 138
Feijoa 17
Felicia 72, 75
Fennel 29
Ferns 86
Fig 86
Forget-me-not 25, 128
fossil log *66*
Francoa 26
Fritillaria persica 'Adiyaman' *22*
Fuchsia 50, *82*, 108, *108*, *111*
    'Violet Gem' *90*
Fulham, London: town garden *32*, 33–4, *35–9*, 142

Galactites 128
Garrya elliptica 'James Roof' *129*
Gentiana sino-ornata 82
Geranium palmatum 51
Gibbs, James: design *8*
Ginger plant *see Zingiber*
Glaucium flavum 126
Gods: ancient 9–10, *11*–12
Golby, Rupert 127–8, 155–7

Halliwell, Brian 71
Hamamelis 127
hanging baskets 94
Hatfield House 113–14
hay racks 65
Hebe 2, 25, 128
Hedera (Ivy) *1*, 40, 67, *88*, 128, *129*, *132*
    helix: 'Glacier' *59*
Hedychium gardnerianum 95
Helianthemum 49
Helichrysum 50, 114
    petiolare 14, 102
Heliotropium 77, 116
    'Chatsworth' *50*, 51, 75
    'Princess Marina' *119*
Helleborus 128, *129*, *132*
    orientalis 134
herbs 18, 26, 49, 80, 94, 99
Hibiscus 113
Hildyard, Isabella 93–4, 149–50
Hildyard, Myles 93–4, 149–50
Hogben, Jane: pots *10*, 34
Holly *6*, 25, *28*, 128
Hosta 86, 113
Howea forsteriana 95
Huntington, Annie 17–18, 139–40
Hyacinth 51
Hydrangea 94, *105*

Ilex (Holly) *6*, 25, *28*, 128
Impatiens 67, *68*, 114, 121
Iresine lindenii 74, *75*
Iris 17, 25
    reticulata 31
Islamic art 9
Italian urns 8–9
Ivy *see Hedera*

Jasmine 94
Jekyll, Gertrude 26, 79
Jewson, Norman 79

Kale 75
Keeling, Jim 8–13, 85–6
Keen, Mary 116
Keim, Gary 121–2, 154–5
knot garden: herbs in 18

Ladder fern 26
Lamium 128
Lavatera 'Barnsley' *70*, 72
lead containers *2*, *8*, *35*, *48*, 78, 79–80, *80*
leaves: on pots 10
Lemon verbena 26, 116
Leycesteria formosa 111
lichen 138
Lilium (Lily) 18, 34, 51, *123*
    'Capitol' *21*
Link, Jim 43
lion: symbolism 10
Lobelia 33, 93
long-tom pots 137
Lotus berthelotii 104
Lychnis coronaria 90
Lysimachia 66, 67

Malahide Castle 113
marble urns *117*
Mathews, J.: orchid pot *42*
Maurandya 26
Melianthus major 51, *70*, 72, 75
Mimulus 114, 137
Monarda 'Sunset' *68*
Morning glory *118*
Munstead House 79
Myrtle 51, 113
mythology 8–10, *11*–13

Nandina 64
Narcissus (Daffodil) 17, *23*, 25, *31*
    'Paper White' *135*
Nash, John 50
Nasturtium 34, 41, 94, 99
Nerine 107
Nerium oleander 17
Nicotiana (Tobacco plant) 51, 113, *123*
Nottinghamshire gardens *92*, 93–4, *95–9*, 149–50

Oenanthe japonica 'Flamingo' *36*
Old Rectory, Burghfield 113–14

ACKNOWLEDGEMENTS

This book would not have been possible without the devoted co-operation of my fifteen contributors and, in many cases, their gardeners, and I would like to thank them all for their enthusiasm and hard work. My thanks also to Andrew Lawson for his great patience when asked to chase across England at 6 am to photograph a single pot of cabbages; to Jerry Harpur for organizing my American contributors and photographing their containers; to Ian Jackson and Elaine Partington at Eddison Sadd for guiding me, relatively painlessly, through the production of this book and listening to my comments; to Barbara Haynes for her great expertise in making sense of some of my late night jottings; to Hilary Krag for painstakingly designing the book; to the staff of The Royal Botanic Gardens, Kew, in identifying the plants which eluded me; and to the Key family of Fibrex Nurseries for their help in identifying various ivies and pelargoniums.

I will always be grateful to the staff at The Royal Horticultural Society's Garden at Wisley and The Royal Botanic Gardens, Kew, for their patience and interest in teaching their students; to Rosemary Verey for helping to launch my freelance career; to my clients for their understanding of my indulgence while this book was being written; and finally to my parents for tolerating the fluctuations in temperament which emanated from my desk.

Editorial Director Ian Jackson
Editor Barbara Haynes
Indexer Dorothy Frame
Art Director Elaine Partington
Art Editor Hilary Krag
Design Assistant Karen Watts
Line-drawing Artist Anthony Duke
Production Hazel Kirkman and
Charles James

All photographs of English gardens are by Andrew Lawson;
photographs of American gardens are by Jerry Harpur.